Teaching the World's Children

ESL for Ages Three to Seven

MARY ASHWORTH

H. PATRICIA WAKEFIELD

Pippin Publishing Limited

Copyright © 1994 by Pippin Publishing Limited
380 Esna Park Drive
Markham, Ontario
L3R 1H5

Edited by Dyanne Rivers
Designed by John Zehethofer
Printed and bound by Kromar Printing Ltd.

Canadian Cataloguing in Publication Data

Ashworth, Mary
    Teaching the world's children : ESL for ages three
to seven

(The Pippin teacher's library ; 16)
Includes bibliographical references.
ISBN 0-88751-062-0

1. English language — Study and teaching as
a second language (Primary).* I. Wakefield, Patricia.
II. Title. III. Series.

PE1128.A2A85 1993   372.65′21′044   C93-094841-6

ISBN 0-88751-062-0

10   9   8   7   6   5   4   3   2   1

CONTENTS

To
Patricia Jane Wakefield
and
Kenneth Foster Reeder
whose dedicated work in the field of language
acquisition by young children is an inspiration
to students, colleagues and friends.

Acknowledgments

We wish to thank the following people who took time to read
and comment on our manuscript:

Jill du Monde
Kenneth Reeder
Judi Ritchie
Victoria Rogers
Jane Wakefield

We would also like to thank the Vancouver School Board and
the Child Study Centre, University of British Columbia, which
allowed us to interview teachers and observe classes in action,
and Dr. R. Jobe, who gave us access to his excellent library of
children's literature from around the world.

Finally, our thanks go to Dyanne Rivers, our editor, for her
wise and sound advice.

. . . .

INTRODUCTION

There was a child went forth every day,
And the first object he look'd upon, that object he became,
And that object became part of him for the day
or a certain part of the day,
Or for many years or stretching cycles of years.

Walt Whitman
Leaves of Grass

Every object a young child encounters, every experience a young child undergoes becomes, as Walt Whitman reminds us, part of that child. As children expand their environment in the magical years between three and seven, these objects and experiences tread closely one upon the other.

If children are to ingest these experiences, they need words—words to describe, expand on and question what they have encountered. No matter what culture they come from or what language they speak, making sense of the world—that is, conceptualizing their experiences—requires language, any language. This language provides them with the symbols to represent the objects and experiences they've absorbed and encountered.

When young children aged three to seven who speak a home language other than English enter an English-speaking school, day care center or preschool, they may be at risk. Suddenly, the flow of comprehensible language they've encountered at home is unavailable and a new and incomprehensible language is substituted in its place. Understanding now becomes very difficult unless early childhood educators know how to create situations in which meaning becomes clear.

Some of these non-English-speaking children are new immigrants; some have been born to immigrant parents living in an English-speaking country. It's common practice in early childhood education to integrate, rather than segregate, children. It's considered more important for children learning English as a second language (ESL) to be exposed to good early childhood education practices than to specific instruction in language. Although there are some very important differences in the way children acquire English as a first and second language, many classroom and center activities work equally well with ESL and English-speaking children, particularly those who seem reluctant to speak out in class. Puppets, for instance, give both the ESL child and the shy English-speaking child a mask to hide behind; it is the puppet who speaks and whose speech is hesitant—the children are safe. We have seen young ESL children who refused to utter a word become quite loquacious once puppets were on their hands.

This book will interest those who work with young children but who are not specialists in teaching ESL. You will find that some background knowledge about learning English as a second language will not only help you understand the young children in your care, but will also make your working lives easier by recognizing that much of what you do with English-speaking children can, occasionally with some modifications, be transferred to ESL children.

Trained ESL specialists do, however, have a part to play in the education of young ESL children. They can withdraw the children from class for a short period each day to work on language, or—and this is preferable—they can work with the child and the teacher in the classroom.

A clarification of terms is necessary to avoid confusion. "Early childhood educator" is a broad term that includes day care workers, as well as preschool, kindergarten and primary teachers. It will be used from time to time, as will the term "teacher," which also refers to anyone in this group. The term "school" or "classroom" refers to any formal learning center; that is, day care centers, preschool groups and school classes. In addition, we've attempted to make our language inclusive by using "he" and "she" at random when the plural "they" is not appropriate.

The chapters that follow intermingle theory and practice. As the axiom says, There is nothing so practical as a good theory. The first chapter outlines the kind of background information teachers need to collect to develop a full understanding of ESL children, the languages they speak, their families and their cultures. The next two chapters talk about language: how children acquire and use it and its role in learning. This is followed by a look at both language and literature as a way of knowing, while the next chapter suggests ways of building bridges to the curriculum, the home, the community and other teachers. "Appendix A—Language" provides a brief overview of how language works and the final chapter, titled "Resources," lists some useful resources and references. Throughout, we try to show how teachers can modify their current teaching methods and materials to accommodate ESL children.

While the book focuses on one group of children, ultimately we must broaden our perspective, recognizing that schools in the '90s are a microcosm of the pluralistic society found in every part of the English-speaking world. Children of the poor and the middle class, children from minority groups and the dominant group are all being educated together. Charles Glenn, writing in the *Phi Delta Kappan* in 1989, challenged educators to stop regarding this mix as a "problem" and begin developing creative ways to make schools fit the children they serve. He advocated:

— that teachers have the same high expectations of all students—poor, middle class and minority.
— that the same support be provided to all students.
— that programs and staff reflect the school population.
— that opportunities to maintain the home language be provided, a policy that sends the message that the first language is valued and respected.
— that schools take seriously the lived culture of minority students and their families, rather than a stereotype.

As we approach the 21st century, the world is becoming smaller and closer. Its joys and sorrows, horrors and achievements, triumphs and tragedies are shared by all of us, young and old, rich and poor. Classrooms are a reflection in microcosm of this pluralistic world and teachers reflect the challenges and frustrations faced by leaders everywhere as we all struggle to make our world a better place. Whether you work in a day care center, a preschool or a school, we hope that you will welcome children from around the globe, that "teaching the world's children" will be a happy and rewarding experience.

WHO ARE

THE CHILDREN?

The more you know about the children in your care and their families, the more you'll be able to help them. While most early childhood educators collect extensive information about all youngsters, it's helpful to have certain additional data on ESL children. It may not be possible, however, to find out everything you want to know immediately. Rather than questioning parents directly, some teachers are more comfortable learning about the children gradually by, for example, using themes such as "Getting to Know You," "Families" or "All about Me."

No matter how it's collected, however, this additional information should be kept on file for continual reference and made available to teachers in subsequent years. It will be just as important and useful when the children are eight or nine years old as it was when it was first recorded.

Adjusting to a new language and culture is a process that takes several years. Furthermore, the information gathered may change significantly as the family adjusts socially and economically. Many immigrant mothers, for example, who have traditionally remained at home as the principal caregiver, may find it necessary to enter the work force for economic reasons. As in any family, this changes the dynamics of daily living and dramatically affects young children in the home. It's important for teachers to be aware of major changes in the children's lives.

Preliminary Information

Collecting information about ESL children is a continuing process that requires constant updating as changes occur. Nevertheless, it's helpful—and, indeed, necessary—to gather some basic information immediately. This can often be done by questioning parents directly, perhaps through an interpreter.

One of the first things to find out is, of course, what languages are spoken in the home. Because the sounds, structures and uses of languages differ, a knowledge of some of the differences between English and a child's home language will assist you in helping the child with aspects of English that seem to cause trouble. The first step in this process is to find out what languages the child speaks or is exposed to.

It's also helpful to know when the child spoke her first word in the native language and whether she now has any trouble speaking the first language. This information is particularly significant if the child is having difficulty learning English. If she was slow to begin speaking her home language, it *may* indicate a language difficulty. At first, parents may be unable—or unwilling—to respond to questions about this. However, as they come to trust you and feel comfortable talking to you, you may be able to add this information to the child's file.

Knowing how a child spends his time at home—what his interests or hobbies are—will provide you with important insights into his experiences with toys, games, story time and household tasks, as well as his relationships with other family members, such as siblings and grandparents. You can use this information as a basis for planning activities such as crafts, food preparation, physical activities, story telling and language experiences for reading and writing.

Teachers can piece together a picture of a child's home life, learning style and behavior expectations by asking questions like, What is the composition of the family circle? Who lives in the home? Who visits frequently? Who is the principal caregiver? and What other family members make decisions that affect the child? The answers to these questions will help you begin planning the bridge between home and school so that the child is able to make a smooth and happy transition.

Answers to your questions about the child's group experiences both within and outside the family, with different age groups, and with the same or opposite sex will provide you with a foundation on which to build more complex group experiences. Language learning is developmental and requires cooperation, participation and communication in a variety of situations. Again, you'll find this information particularly helpful as you plan activities based on what the child already knows or can do.

When planning a child's program, teachers need to know whether the home can—or will—reinforce the English learned at school and support the child by displaying a positive attitude towards both the English language and the culture of the school. At the same time, it's important for teachers to support parents' efforts to maintain the child's first language and culture. If these don't continue to develop, she will be deprived of cognitive and literacy development in her home language, pride in her heritage and an important medium of communication with family members.

Teachers need to be very aware of and sensitive to the decisions about language and culture parents must make as they settle in a new country. These decisions profoundly affect who the child is and who he will become. As Basil Bernstein pointed out, "If the culture of the teacher is to become part of the consciousness of the child, then the culture of the child must first be in the consciousness of the teacher."

Where Do They Come from?

The factors that make people who they are and influence who they become is the essence of the nature versus nurture debate. We are all affected by our genetic background and the capabilities and limitations we were born with. Just as influential, however, is the environment in which we develop and grow—family, peers, school and neighborhood. The interaction between these elements, nature and nurture, is the crucial factor that determines the essence of every individual.

CULTURE

All families transmit "culture" to their children. The culture transmitted is influenced by the family's socio-economic background and by the religious beliefs and educational, political and social values of the parents or principal caregivers. The family interprets for the child its system of values, beliefs and

15

ideas about appropriate behavior by establishing a framework that socializes children so that they may become active participants, first in the family and, later, in the larger community. The framework is the same for all families; that is, they all establish certain patterns of communication and interaction, as well as routines, customs and expectations for behavior.

These practices vary among cultures. Because most parents tend to bring up their children as they were brought up, there is a continuity in the transmission of family culture that, in our multicultural society, results in a dazzling array of approaches and beliefs.

All children bring to the day care center or school the culture of the home and take home the culture of the center or school. An important element of the teacher's role is to understand and mediate between the two so that the child's view of the world continues to develop smoothly. While unresolved conflicts are destructive and counter-productive, an understanding of different viewpoints can often be reached through friendly discussion.

Taking a culturally sensitive approach to all children is an acquired skill, built up over time by teachers who are willing to listen, seek out information and interact with the community.

Finding out about a child's home culture—family roles and relationships, communication techniques, customs and routines—provides teachers with important insights into cultural similarities and differences in child-rearing practices. The following sections outline the kind of information that it's helpful to seek out. When you question parents about these things, their answers may not be simple or definitive. The information gleaned, however, can be gradually augmented through experience, continual interaction with parents and members of the community, and by reading some of the many books and articles that are available.

As teachers and ESL children and families struggle to adjust to new cultures and to each other, a variety of factors must be considered. To enable them to reassess strategies and procedures from year to year, many teachers record their observations and insights in journals. As your experience with immigrant families increases, your strategies will continue to evolve and you'll refine your own ideas about the kind of information that's helpful.

16

Relationships and Communication

The Western concept of the nuclear family is often unfamiliar to new immigrants. For this reason, it's helpful to understand the role of the mother, father, siblings and the extended family in child-rearing. In their native countries, grandparents and even uncles and aunts often live in the same quarters, playing an active role in child-rearing and participating in decisions that affect the child. It may not be unusual for the whole family or for an uncle or aunt to come to the school to register the child.

At first, finding out about the family's fundamental approach to child-rearing may be difficult. In some cases, parents may be unable—or unwilling—to express their ideas; in others, they may not be consciously aware of their beliefs. Culture is learned and transmitted unconsciously. For example, in most Southeast Asian cultures, there are no social occasions at which children are not welcomed. In addition, according to Itty Chan, the concept of the "social self" rather than the "individual self" is crucial to child-rearing in many Asian cultures. In other words, the child's relationship to those around him is more important than the development of his individuality. Because these attitudes and ideas are the norm in these cultures, keep in mind that it may not occur to parents to mention them to you.

Children begin learning as soon as they're born. While this learning is spontaneous and irregular, it is also focused and meaningful. Because children's first learning styles are formed in the home according to the customs and beliefs prevalent in the surrounding culture, it's helpful for teachers to know how ESL children learn at home. For example, do they learn by listening and watching? By being asked questions? By asking questions? If the teaching style of the early childhood educator differs greatly from the learning style of the child, confusion and frustration may result. When necessary, wise teachers will adapt their teaching style until individual children are ready to shift to other ways of learning.

In some cultures, children's first responsibility is to the home, not the school. This means that if there is work to be done on the land or in the store, or if a younger child is ill, an older child may be kept home to help. Children may also be kept home to observe a holy day. It is also not uncommon for some families to visit their homelands for two or three months during the school year. All these factors can influence a child's attendance record. Teachers or bilingual home-school workers may be called upon to explain attendance regulations to parents, emphasizing the importance of regular attendance and punctuality at school to ensure the continuity of the child's education.

Customs

Because the meaning of gestures and other forms of non-verbal communication differs from culture to culture, misinterpretations can cause misunderstandings or embarrassment. In Vietnam, for example, the gesture we use to mean "come here" is used only with animals. In another part of the world, shaking the head means "yes," not "no." In some cultures, it's considered bad manners for children to look adults in the eye when speaking to them. Of course, teachers cannot learn all the non-verbal language of all the cultures they will encounter. Nevertheless, a knowledge of the meaning of some gestures and body language and a willingness to learn about and respect others will help establish a bond between teacher, child and family.

In some cases, parents from other cultures may be shocked at the way North American children dress for school. They may equate a tidy child with decency and a respect for education. For others, some aspects of dress have religious significance; for example, a young Sikh boy may wear his long hair tied up on top of his head in a *jurra*. When this is the case, parents may understandably insist upon retaining certain dress customs in the new country. Teachers can help children avoid ridicule by explaining the significance of their dress to other children and by modeling by example respect for differences.

Food is a wonderful common denominator among all people. Favorite foods are fun to share; new foods can be an adventure. Of course, children should never be offered foods that are forbidden at home. For the knowledgeable teacher, one who is interested in finding out things like which foods are taboo and which are favorites, which are unknown in the new culture and which constitute a child's main diet, learning about foods can be the source of many teachable moments and pleasant sharing experiences that may involve activities such as shopping for, preparing, cooking, presenting and eating various foods.

All children love celebrations. They are delighted when a festival important to them is incorporated into the school routine. It gives them the opportunity to be the "knowers" and to share their special knowledge with others. In turn, this gives the other children the opportunity to have a new experience that they can share at home. Creative teachers can turn a knowledge of the kinds of family customs and rituals that are celebrated in other cultures into a feast of learning experiences using creative activities such as art, music or drama. Children can be encouraged to broaden their food experiences by tasting and smelling unknown foods, by making meals, and by learning about ingredients, while others can enlarge their cultural experiences through hearing stories, talking to visitors, and viewing pictures and films. Newcomers can share their knowledge with other children in the school through class exchanges, by contributing to school or community newspapers, and through dramatic performances.

In Western culture, play is considered essential to children's growth and development. It is an important medium through which children learn. Many cultures, however, do not share this perspective: sand boxes, water tables, games, puppets, dramatic play and field trips are viewed as non-essential, important only for their entertainment value. Some parents view schools as places where children should sit at desks and learn reading, writing and mathematics.

Perceptions like this are cultural and will not change overnight. It's helpful, then, for teachers to be aware of things like the games ESL children play at home, with whom they play at home and at school, and the emphasis parents place on the value of play. If parents disapprove of play at school, teachers should try to help them understand another point of view. A good starting point is to ask them about the games their children play at home, then follow up by teaching these games from other countries to all the children in the group. In future discussions with parents, teachers can comment on the shared games and point out the skills the children learned from them.

Routines at Home

All families establish routines, repetitive procedures that streamline day-to-day family life and satisfy basic human needs.

These routines form an important part of the child's day at home. Because additional routines will be established at school, it's important for teachers to know what has gone before. It's also helpful to know how rigidly these are enforced. Encourage parents and children to describe the routines—the mealtime, bedtime, dressing and personal hygiene rituals—that are an important element of their family life. It will be helpful to find out things like:

— Who is present at mealtimes?
— Who talks? What about? Are children welcomed to the conversation?
— What variations occur at breakfast, lunch, dinner and snacktime?
— Does the child have an afternoon nap?
— When is bedtime? Is it strictly enforced?
— Are stories read or told at bedtime?
— Does the child wash and brush his teeth? By himself or with help?
— What time does the child get up?
— Does she dress herself or does she need help?
— Does the child keep his room tidy?
— If you're dealing with a very young child, it may be necessary to ask if she is toilet-trained.

Expectations

If a child's transition from home to school is to be effected smoothly, teachers and parents must cooperate and exchange information. Parents need to know what to expect from the child's experiences at school, and teachers need to know what the child is building on.

Even when children are entering their second, third and fourth years of schooling and therefore have some past school experience to refer to, it's important for their teachers to be aware of parental expectations. The more teachers know about the children, the more effective they can make the teaching and learning situation.

The story of John, a seven-year-old who had been in a school situation since he was four, is an example of how this can work successfully. At school, John seemed unable to keep anything organized. His written work was messy and his papers crumpled. Although he always arrived at school neatly dressed, he often misplaced articles of clothing during the day. When he took a storybook home, it nearly always got lost.

A conversation with his mother revealed that John was the only child of a late marriage. His parents showed their love for him by showering him with attention. He wasn't expected to dress himself, keep his room tidy or take any responsibility for his belongings. His mother tried to anticipate his every wish. In her culture, boys—and men—are waited on and are not expected to take any responsibility for household matters.

Over the course of several conversations, the teacher and the mother worked together to help John meet the expectations of the school by developing strategies to encourage him to become independent and responsible. Within six weeks, the improvement in his classroom behavior was marked and all three—mother, child and teacher—were happier.

Teachers need to know things like:

— What kinds of behavior are valued most in the child's family?
— How is inappropriate behavior dealt with?
— When are children expected to begin taking some responsibility for household tasks? For their personal appearance? For keeping their belongings tidy?
— Are expectations of boys different from those of girls?
— What expectations do parents have of the school?
— What aspirations do they have for their children?

Routines and Procedures at Day Care Centers and Schools

Parents' cooperation in reinforcing school or day care center routines is helpful and can often be enlisted if they are aware of these from the first day their child attends. Depending on the situation, it may be necessary to communicate these verbally through an interpreter or translate them in writing. It's a good idea to cover issues like the following:

— Fee scales, if any, and payment procedures.

- The time the class starts and stops and the days the center is open if it isn't Monday through Friday.
- Whether the children can be cared for before and after school if both parents work; whether the child will be picked up after school and by whom.
- The forms, such as registration forms or permission slips for field trips or inoculations, that must be filled out.
- Procedures to be followed if a child is too sick to go to school, or if a child meets with an accident at school.
- Who should be contacted—at home and at school—in case of an emergency.
- Whether children should bring snacks or lunch money.
- Additional clothes children might need for some activities; e.g., a T-shirt and shorts for physical education or a long shirt to use as a coverall for art.
- Other supplies that should be brought from home.

Adjusting Your Classroom

The following are suggestions for helping children and parents adapt to the new culture, the school system and the community. While these suggestions are very important for teachers receiving ESL children new to the school or day care setting, they are also useful even when these children have settled in to their second or third years of school. Adjustment is a gradual process; it takes years rather than months.

- Set up a buddy system for the children, first using someone who speaks their language, and later an English-speaking buddy. This technique is useful well beyond the initial stages of adjustment. In fact, a buddy system can be used with the whole class. For example, older children can be paired with younger children for shared reading, projects, experiments and field trips.
- When children enter the system, arrange for them to become familiar with the school and its environment. Conducting a tour of the school may be the buddy's first assignment.
- Do not overwhelm the child at first with too much material or too many toys. Some children may have never seen such an array of materials. For those who

have attended school in their own countries, the bright colors of your classroom and the multitude of materials may come as a shock.

— Don't hurry the ESL child! Most prefer to watch classroom activities quietly for a while. Some will join in gradually, while others may remain silent for some time. It's important, however, for the teacher to show awareness of the child's presence—talk to him often, smile at him frequently, and draw his attention to new things. This will help avoid the unpleasant feeling recalled by many older ESL students— the sense that they were "invisible" at this stage of their adjustment.

— Capitalize on the skills children already possess. They may not know how to use scissors but they may be very adept at, for example, creating objects out of modeling dough. Buddies or an aide can show them how to use scissors and, in return, the ESL children might make something out of the dough.

— Encourage the children to play in the imaginary or dramatic play area so that you can observe the roles they like to take.

— Reward culturally appropriate behavior and try to ignore what is inappropriate at first. Remember, behavior that is unacceptable in the classroom may be perfectly acceptable in the child's home, a situation that is sometimes confusing for children. Help the child make the transition from home to school and vice versa by being firm, gentle and persistent.

— Invite parents to visit your classroom often, with an interpreter if necessary. Make sure they understand that they are partners in their child's education. Some parents may appreciate an invitation to participate in classroom activities.

— Listen with respect and careful attention to what parents tell you. There will be areas of disagreement. Try to find a resolution but, if this is not possible, respect the parents' opinions.

— While visiting the child's home may benefit you, the child and the parents, it may be wise to wait a few weeks before suggesting the idea.

- If you need information about the cultural practices of a particular group, try to consult either a bilingual home-school worker or a member of the ethnic group.
- If children seem underclad, undernourished or over-tired, seek help from the school counselor or community nurse immediately. Parents may be having difficulty, financially or otherwise, finding the right clothes or buying the foods they're used to. They may need and welcome some assistance or direction.
- Incorporate into your curriculum lessons designed to teach about foods, nutrition and clothing.
- Watch for signs of stress. Although most children are resilient about accepting change, there are some who react to pressure by acting out or withdrawing, both physically and mentally. Seek professional help imme-diately.
- Never permit children's behavior or dress to be ridi-culed by other children or teachers. Act as an advocate for ESL children by showing others that, while there are many similarities among people of all races, it is the differences that delight and enrich all of us.

HOW CHILDREN ACQUIRE

AND USE LANGUAGE

A newborn baby is totally dependent on the caregiver for all her needs which, in the early weeks, appear to be predominantly physical—the need to be fed and the need to be kept warm and dry. If these needs are not satisfied, the baby cries. But there is another need that must also be satisfied—the baby must hear talk. This talk, which includes talk to the baby and talk among the adults and other children around her, becomes part of her environment.

Akbar the Great, the Mogul emperor who lived from 1542 to 1605, believed that if babies were not allowed to hear human voices, they would grow up unable to speak. To test his theory, he had a small house for newborn babies built on the grounds of his palace. The babies were fed and cared for but heard no speech. At four years of age, they were, as Akbar had predicted, unable to speak.

Learning the First Language

Research has established that as early as one month after birth and possibly earlier, a baby begins to distinguish among and respond to the myriad sounds around him. A mother's voice soothes and elicits certain kinds of coos and whimpers from the baby. Rapidly, these sounds become responses first to physical needs such as hunger, wetness or pain and later to the music of the surrounding language. Very young children internalize the sounds, the intonation and the patterns of words they will need in order to function in their environment.

During the first six months of life, the sounds made by babies anywhere in the world are remarkably similar. Some theorists believe that, as babies grow, they gradually screen out sounds that are not reinforced by the surrounding caregivers. Other more recent research claims that babies can distinguish their home tongue four days after birth. At any rate, it's clear that, in a very short time, babies begin to demonstrate their aptitude for learning language.

The strategies used by caregivers in providing experiences and stimulating responses affect the baby's developing language and ability to communicate. Some caregivers accompany daily rituals such as bathing, changing and feeding with a steady stream of talk. Gradually, young children learn that pauses in this talk can be filled with their own responses. And so the art of conversation is initiated.

For parents, the moment when an infant takes her first steps, throws an object or puts objects into her mouth or a container is filled with excitement. This excitement rises when they're able to distinguish a few meaningful words amid her babble of sounds, usually sometime after the child's first birthday. For the next few months, the child will usually add one word at a time to her vocabulary. Once about fifty words are acquired, she'll begin to put two or three words together to form rudimentary sentences.

Researchers have provided some fascinating insights into the nature of these first utterances. They are distinctive in three ways:

— The word or utterance has a distinctive phonetic form; that is, the "word" sounds the same in whatever context it's used. It may be an approximation of an adult word, such as /muk/ for "milk," or it may have a phonetic form that makes sense only to the child; for example, /lo/ for "elephant" or /dee/ for "horse."

— The meaning of the utterance is clear to the child but it may not initially have the same meaning for an adult. For example, the child may use "ball" to identify any round object, whether it's a radish, a roll of toilet paper or an orange, or call all four-legged animals "doggie."

— The context in which a word is used may indicate that the child is giving it several different meanings. For example, the word "mommy" may be used to call, name, comment on, look for or demand something. The intonation pattern is usually a clue.

A brief overview of some linguistic terms is found in "Appendix A—Language" on page 79.

The question "What's that?" seems to herald a period of rapid vocabulary growth as children discover that it's the key to acquiring all kinds of information about the world around them. This stage is termed the "naming explosion" by many researchers.

As children acquire more words and learn to combine them meaningfully to express their needs and comment on their surroundings, it's evident that they are using strategies for organizing their thoughts. They may use some kinds of words, such as nouns, verbs and adjectives, but not others, such as articles, conjunctions and prepositions. They seldom use plurals or verb endings. Although this speech is simple, it is genuinely creative; that is, the utterances are neither repetitions nor simplifications of adult speech. They are unique. For example, a child commenting on her dislike of noisy firecrackers at Halloween may say, "No way bang."

Physical development, too, reflects children's growing confidence in their ability to manage their world. This may include valiant efforts to put on socks and shoes without help, an insistence on feeding themselves, creating towers, trains and houses out of blocks, arranging doll furniture and naming toy animals. Although there is still a great deal of parallel play, there is a growing interest in other children and definite attempts at cooperative play.

From this time on, children become prolific talkers. Their talk is often used to initiate activities or a social exchange with caregivers. Their experience with language is augmented by listening to others and responding to their caregivers' attempts to encourage them to extend their statements. Here's an example:

Child: See plane.
Adult: Yes, there's a plane up in the sky.
Child: Up sky. Vroom, vroom.
Adult: I wonder where it's going. Do you think it's going to

Spain?
Child: Yeah, Spain. I went to Spain.
Adult: Yes, you did. Did you go in an airplane?
Child: Yes, and Mommy comed and Daddy and you.

They also augment their own language experiences by listening to adult conversations in which they are not active participants.

Interest in books and in being read to also increases at this stage. This interest is often reflected in imaginative and dramatic play, as children assign roles or characteristics to their playthings.

Between the ages of three and five, children become quite independent physically. They can run and jump, go up and down stairs, ride a tricycle, swing, slide, throw a ball and dress themselves. Correspondingly, speech is not as centered in the here and now, but combines running commentary with action.

Children do not talk merely for the sake of talking. Speech is a tool they use to think, to get things done, to enlist help, to obtain the things they want, to comment on and share experiences, and to participate in activities.

In his book, *The Meaning Makers*, Gordon Wells pointed out that, as young children are learning to talk, they increasingly use talk to learn about other things. Four-year-olds are notorious questioners. Surely there is not a caregiver alive who has not been exasperated by the sheer volume of requests for information and the relentlessly recurring "Why?" This is how children use language to learn, processing the information they receive to modify and refine their own view of the world.

Perhaps the most fascinating way that children use language to explore and expand their knowledge of the world is through imaginary play. Most children at this stage willingly engage in "pretend" activities with other children, adults and even by themselves. They freely use past experiences, substitutions, predictions and conjecture. The world they create is vivid, exciting and engrossing. The language that expresses this world is a window through which adults can observe and participate in the child's expanding viewpoint. Here, for example, is what one four-year-old asked her mother after reading a Chinese folktale involving a princess named Purest Joy:

Child: Can I have some perfume on?
Mother: Why?
Child: 'Cause I want to be beautiful with Purest Joy. I am obviously a princess.

The transition from home to school, whether it occurs at a preschool or in kindergarten or grade one, marks an important turning point in terms of language development. At home, children develop both their physical and conversational skills in unstructured circumstances. The greater part of their experience is often with one caregiver. Even when more than one is involved, the number is usually limited and they are delighted to focus exclusively on the child. Learning, although it is spontaneous and unstructured, is nevertheless steady and involving for the child.

The function of schools is to broaden children's range of experiences, introduce new possibilities, systematize the process of learning, help develop thinking skills and, ultimately, empower students to take responsibility for their own learning. The strategies children have developed at home to make sense of their world, to talk about their experiences and to wonder about what is new or imaginary continue to be effective. These strategies should not be supplanted by the school but augmented by teachers skilled in helping all children discover their potential.

Gordon Wells told us that knowledge cannot be transmitted in isolation, but must be reinvented as the learner brings to each new situation his own previous experience and background and interprets new information from that perspective. By the time children come to school, they are already successful communicators. They know what language is for and how to use it competently. As they experience new situations and interact with new adults and children, they continue to use language to interpret, ask questions, negotiate, comment and wonder. With skillful guidance from and the understanding of teachers, children's language continues to grow and blossom in the school environment.

"Meaning-making in conversation is a collaborative activity," Gordon Wells wrote. The wise early childhood teacher knows how to create an atmosphere in which children's experiences outside school are valued and talked about, where their ideas and comments are listened to with respect, and where they learn to reflect on what they know. Language is the key to creative thinking, solving problems and collaborative learning. The growth and development of language is a lifelong activity, an essential component of successful living.

Learning a Second Language

Although they may not be able to express themselves in English very well, the young ESL children you are meeting for the first time are, in fact, experienced language users. Cognitively and linguistically, they are as well-developed as their English-speaking counterparts, but this development has taken place in another language and culture. Now they must begin the process of transferring what they know to a new context and continuing their development in two languages.

First, however, here are some facts about language that it's important to keep in mind:

— *Language is a human universal.* All cultural groups have a language system that their members master in order to communicate with each other.
— *Language is systematic.* Every language has its own characteristic way of combining sounds, words and sentences.
— *No language is wholly regular.* Exceptions to the rule are found in all languages.
— *All languages enable speakers to create new utterances.* However, these utterances must conform to the rules established over the centuries by speakers of a particular language.
— *Language is both creative and functional.* A speaker of any language can both create and comprehend an infinite number of utterances based on a finite number of rules. These utterances can cover a multitude of functions, such as requesting, refusing, promising, warning, denying, agreeing, disagreeing and expressing emotions.
— *Languages change.* For example, new words can be created to meet the scientific and technological demands of the modern world.
— *Human beings have an innate capacity to learn language.* All children, unless they are severely neurologically impaired, are capable of learning a language.

— *Language can be non-verbal as well as verbal.* Facial expressions, gestures and other body movements may convey messages, the meanings of which are culturally specific.
— *Language and culture are closely related.* Customs, traditions, values, stories, religion, history and other manifestations of culture are transmitted to a large extent through language.
— *Language and thought are closely related.* Children and adults use language to share their thoughts and to expand and clarify concepts.

Although there are many similarities between the way first and second languages are acquired, there are also important differences that cannot be ignored.

Young English-speaking children don't know another language; ESL children do. They've mastered many of the skills involved in listening and talking. They know what language is and how to use it to request, demand, invite, socialize and much more.

All young children are highly motivated to learn language. Surrounded by love and attention, encouraged and complimented for all their vocal efforts, they continually make every attempt to communicate. Children learning a second language, however, may not feel the same urgency to communicate in English as their English-speaking counterparts. They can already make themselves understood in their home language. Their initial efforts to speak English at school may be met not with praise and encouragement, but with misunderstanding and ridicule. In addition, they may hear English only at school, never at home, so that their exposure to comprehensible input is limited.

When young children attempt to use language at home, their adult caregivers try very hard to understand the meaning of their utterances and pay little attention to its form. For ESL children, the opposite is too often true. When they attempt to use English at school, the teacher often pays more attention to the form than to the message.

Young children learn their home language slowly over a number of years. There is no pressure; every advance is enthusiastically welcomed. When it becomes necessary for ESL children to learn English to communicate at school, the atmosphere is very different. There is considerable pressure on them to learn the new language quickly. This pressure doesn't necessarily come from the teacher, but may originate with other children, the school system and their parents. Encouragement of children's efforts should include praise for making progress, which is often phenomenal.

Concepts and language development go hand in hand. All young children develop concepts of shape and color at an early age. Some of these ideas transfer easily into another language. Others, however, are different and can cause confusion. For example, the color spectrum is not divided the same way in all cultures. Yellow and green are separated by vocabulary into two colors in English; in some other cultures, one word describes that range of color. On the other hand, there are some notable similarities that help teachers as they plan activities. For example, the concept of round—a circle—is universal; only the vocabulary is different.

All children need to hear English modeled by both adults and their peers in a variety of situations. In both languages, there is a role for imitation. Although all the phonemes, or sounds (see "Appendix A"), of English are not found in other languages and vice versa, all children benefit from activities that highlight different combinations of sounds. For example, in the song, "Old Macdonald Had a Farm," each verse introduces a new animal sound. In English, the cow says, "A moo-moo here, and a moo-moo there." But this approximation of animal sounds is not the same in all languages. A Chinese cow, for example, says, "Woo."

All children need to play with language, try it out, test it, receive feedback and try again. This is the way children test the rules and adjust them to their own world view, a process that prevails among all language learners.

All children need to have adult language adjusted to their level of understanding and, finally, all children learn faster when language and content are combined. Language is a tool for learning.

Principles and Their Application

There is certainly no shortage of theories to explain how children acquire a second language. Some of them have little significance for very young children; others, though now out-of-date, have left in their wake some gems of wisdom that are useful in any classroom.

It is not the purpose of this book to provide detailed theoretical descriptions of second language teaching methodologies. Instead, this section presents several principles that guide second language teaching and that all teachers can incorporate into their daily programs.

Each principle is followed by a classroom application that demonstrates how theory and practice can be combined to create an atmosphere that encourages and supports continuous language learning.

Children learning English as a second language are, first of all, children.

All children need a sense of self-esteem, a warm accepting atmosphere and friends around them. They need to experience success and have many opportunities to explore and discover. When planning classroom activities, keep in mind that ESL children have knowledge of another language and culture that others, including you, may not. If you can find a way to use and recognize this, perhaps by teaching everyone to say a greeting, sing a song or play a game in another language, the ESL child will have a much-needed opportunity to be the "knower."

Encourage new friendships by pairing English-speaking and ESL children to explore a concept, such as matching, play a game or complete a task, such as delivering something to the office. Communication will develop naturally among children who are busily engaged in cooperative activities. It's more important to pay attention to ESL children's need to feel accepted and valued than to their level of proficiency in the second language.

Like learning a first language, learning a second language does not progress in a linear series of well-defined stages.

When learning a first language, children develop their own world view and the language that goes with it. As their world expands, so does the language needed to cope with it. The language used by a child may be very mature in some respects and immature in others. This language reflects the central core of children's understanding and changes with their need to express their understanding of concepts.

Children learn a second language so they can use it with their friends. They are not interested in language as anything but a means of communication.

Young ESL children do not learn language by being subjected to drills. They learn language because they need it for something. This might be to make a request, as in the following example:

ESL Child (Pointing): Truck.
Teacher: You want the fire truck?
ESL Child: Want fire truck.
Teacher: Kuldip wants the fire truck. Jimmy, can Kuldip have a turn?

They may also use language to invite or respond to an invitation, as follows:

English-Speaking Child: Wanna play?
ESL Child: Okay. You be father. I'm baby.
English-Speaking Child: No, I want to be the baby.
ESL Child: Okay. I make dinner.

Sometimes ESL children learn a chunk of language, such as "Bye teacher. See you tomorrow," that they can use in a specific context. At other times, a child may focus on details of grammar or vocabulary. For example, after noticing that we say "slowly," he may ask why we don't also say "fastly." The language children learn is the language they use.

Language develops best when it's learned in a variety of contexts and when content is varied.

ESL children learn English more quickly when they're engaged in activities that interest them, in which they're eager to participate and in which they must interact with English-speakers. Children learn best through play, games, make-believe, storytelling and songs. Both the context and the content of the activities need to be varied, holding the children's interest and giving them the opportunity to participate at their own level.

A single school day can include activities like art, storytelling or reading, games to encourage the development of both small- and gross-motor coordination, songs, snack preparation and imaginative play. Occasional activities can include field trips, class exchanges and dramatic performances.

Literacy is a part of language. Therefore reading and writing, along with listening and speaking, need to be developed from the beginning.

Providing name tags, labeling objects around the classroom, and combining pictures with print are techniques that help all children grasp the concept that print represents meaning. In most classrooms, these things are part of the environment. With ESL children in particular, the relationship between meaning and the printed word needs to be emphasized and expanded throughout all the early childhood years.

The teacher needs to keep in mind that, compared to English-speaking children, ESL children have been exposed to the sounds of English for only a short time. As a result, they will not be ready to begin developing their skill at relating sounds to visual representations, such as matching words and pictures and recognizing sight words, at the same time as their English-speaking counterparts. They do, however, need to be exposed to this process so they have the freedom to begin when they're ready.

Just as it does for English-speaking children, writing can begin immediately for ESL children. A scribble on artwork may not be a meaningful signature to the teacher or other children, but if it's the child's own interpretation, it is authentic. She will adjust the representation over time, just as she does her oral language.

All children need to be read to every day. This is perhaps the most enjoyable way for children to learn so-called literary language and about how a story is constructed, as well as to expand their world through imagination and wonder. It will not be long before phrases like "Once upon a time..." and "...happily ever after," will be heard in imaginative play.

The four skills of language—listening, speaking, reading and writing—should be interwoven into the activities of every integrated day. The interplay among the skills augments the children's grasp of language so that they can express their expanding knowledge more clearly.

. . . .

THE ROLE OF LANGUAGE

IN LEARNING

Each of us has internalized a mosaic of concepts. Concepts are thoughts, ideas and opinions; they are generalizations formed over the years on the basis of our particular experiences; they are notions about things and practices and about how they work. Some concepts are universal; some culture-bound. We all construct our own individual representation of the world as we experience it and, from this, we generate our expectations. What is fixed in our consciousness is there for us to return to, and perhaps modify in the light of new experiences.

How Concepts Develop

Children develop concepts as they learn to deal intelligently with the world around them. As they absorb ideas, first in the home and, later, at school, they build their world view. Concepts allow them to organize their perceptions of their environment and adjust this world view as new experiences are added.

Before young ESL children enter a preschool group, they will already have acquired many concepts on the basis of their personal experiences at home. The concepts they learn in preschool and in the early grades of school may reinforce and extend the concepts they've learned at home—or, in some cases, they may appear to contradict them because some concepts, such as the classification of colors or vegetables, differ among cultures. Concepts that appear to be contradictory are neither superior nor inferior—just different. It is, however, important that children learn the concepts of the dominant culture as well as those of their home culture, so that they may move comfortably between the two cultures if they so choose.

When ESL children enter an early childhood program, they will both develop new concepts and transfer concepts they have already learned. To transfer previously learned concepts, they need English words. New concepts are often consciously and deliberately taught by the teacher and arise out of a combination of language (with words and phrases repeated several times) and teacher-directed manipulation of the immediate environment. Language and thought are very closely related—each stimulates the other, making it possible for teachers to give young children the opportunity to continue their cognitive development as they learn English.

In the past, it was thought that ESL children should be isolated from the mainstream until they acquired a degree of basic fluency in English. Today, young ESL children are nearly always integrated into classes with their peer groups. Although they do need extra support both in teaching and materials, they thrive on today's curriculum: a systematic, sequential presentation of concepts with the language necessary to express them and the reasoning strategies necessary to expand and modify them. In every case, these are geared to the developmental capabilities of individual children.

To sum up, here are nine valuable principles that can be applied directly in classrooms:

Concepts depend on perceptions that are taken in by all the senses.

Classroom activities should employ as many of the senses as possible. Some children learn better through one sense than another.

Children develop language and concepts as they interact with adults and other children.

Talking should not only be encouraged but also specifically planned for. Depending on their age and language ability, children can be paired or placed in small groups to undertake a challenging task with or without an adult.

Some concepts are universal; some culture-bound.

Concepts that are culture-bound, such as the number of colors that make up the rainbow, sometimes differ from culture to culture. As a result, ESL children may find them contradictory.

Language and thought are interdependent and mutually stimulating.

Both inside and outside the classroom, ESL children need an environment that encourages exploration and talking. Interaction with the community, interesting materials, field trips, and frequent visitors are essential components of a good program.

Concepts also lie at the heart of social relations and value systems, and these vary among cultures.

Teaching bilingualism means teaching biculturalism, one important aspect of which is social behavior. Teachers can become culture conscious so that they are more sensitive to children's adjustment needs.

Concepts learned in the home often begin with the experience and move to the word. Concepts learned in school often begin with the word and move to the experience.

ESL children entering an English-speaking school may need to develop a new way of learning. In some cultures, young children watch and listen, then experiment. The words come later. As they grow older, they may encounter the language before—or at the same time as—they undergo the experience. It may be necessary to direct the children's attention to the language used by the teacher and other children, as well as to their own use of English.

As children advance through the grades at school, learning increasingly depends on their ability to use words as symbols.

Children must be helped to move from the concrete to the abstract mode of expression if they are to compete on equal terms with their peers in high school; that is, they must be encouraged to use words, rather than gestures or actions, to describe objects, events, ideas and past, present and future experiences.

Learning also depends on children's command of complex sentence structures and words that describe processes and show relationships.

Teachers should carefully monitor ESL children's language to ensure that they are gradually learning and using the sentence structures and vocabulary needed for abstract thought. In addition, teachers should not only create situations that require them to use words like "how," "why," and "because," but also model for the children the expressions they need.

Learning a concept is not a one-shot deal!

Children need a variety of experiences with a concept in a variety of situations with a variety of people. Each new experience will result in some modification, extension or limitation of the concept.

The following are some of the clusters of concepts that young children should become familiar with over time:

— *Identification* of objects beginning with those that are immediate and personal, such as body parts, clothing and objects in the classroom.

— *Classification* according to color, shape, size, number, function and kind, again beginning with what is immediate, personal and concrete; comparing and contrasting these.

— *Spatial relationships*, such as "near" and "far," "in front of" and "behind" and "under" and "over." In every classroom, opportunities abound for both the informal and formal teaching of spatial relationships. For example, activities such as games, handicrafts and tidying up can all involve opportunities to develop children's awareness of spatial relationships.

— *Temporal relationships*, such as past, present and future, "before" and "after," and "since" and "during." Because time is less concrete than space, it represents an increased level of difficulty for some children. Some aspects of time, such as attitudes towards the future or the keeping of appointments, are culture-bound.

— *Emotional and familial relationships*, such as love and hate, happiness and unhappiness, loyalty, family, kinship, self and others, including both other children and adults. Many of these concepts are culture-bound. In North America, for example, far more emphasis is placed on the individual than on the group. As another example, some cultures differentiate between an uncle on the mother's side and an uncle on the father's side. Unless teachers are aware of these differences, they may confuse the children.

— *Ordering*, which can evolve from one of the other concept clusters. For example, items that have been classified as big or little can be arranged in order from biggest to littlest or yesterday's field trip can be reviewed in chronological sequence by talking about what the class did first, next, and so on.

— *Equivalency*, which involves recognizing that, although things may differ in some respects, they may, in fact, be the same—or equivalent—in others. For example, different shapes may enclose the same area or different-shaped vessels may contain the same amount of liquid. Practical experience with containers of the same or different size helps develop the concept of equivalency.

Emergent Literacy

Emergent literacy, a term coined by Marie Clay in 1966 to describe how young children gradually become aware of the uses of written language in their environment, has been widely used in educational literature for only the past decade. This ever-increasing awareness of writing and reading is now considered an integral part of children's early language development.

Before this theory emerged, researchers thought language development in the early years was only a precursor to the acquisition of the essential skills of reading, encoding and decoding. It was widely believed that the so-called readiness skills (letter recognition, recognition of the sound-symbol correspondence, etc.) that preceded the act of reading could be taught only when children were developmentally and physically ready to absorb them. This readiness, it was believed, occurred as a result of maturation after children began formal schooling and were ready to be taught the specific skills that would enable them to read.

As linguists conducted research that led them to realize that a cognitive model was far more productive in explaining language acquisition than a stimulus-response model, development in the early childhood years began to receive more attention. Researchers such as Marie Clay and William Teale began to describe what they called early reading behaviors in children younger than school age. Researchers already understood that young children were active participants in learning language as they used it to generate hypotheses and solve problems. In the presence of print, young children independently investigated the relationship between oral and written language. Studies repeatedly showed that young children paid attention to both writing and reading and that all four modes of language—listening, speaking, reading and writing—seemed to develop in a parallel fashion.

Young children who grow up in a literate society learn to use written language naturally as they interact socially with the adults in their environment. They become familiar with some of the functions of literacy as they observe how written language is used to get things done. For example, they learn that books are for reading, for listening to stories, for looking at pictures, for enjoying a comfortable social exchange with an adult, and that labels, signs and logos are for giving information and for relating print and object to meaning. They know that the golden arches represent McDonald's, that a calendar tells them when their birthday is, that a list tells Mommy what to buy at the store, and that the marks they make on paper with a pencil or pen can represent whatever they want them to in oral language. Most children are very willing to interpret their drawings or scribbles to an adult willing to listen.

The results of this renewed interest by researchers in early childhood development has resulted in some very important changes in the way we look at the acquisition of language, particularly written language. It is now generally accepted that children's thinking processes are qualitatively different from those of adults. Preschool children have not mastered the conventions of written language but they know that it is an integral part of their world, that it is useful to them in many ways, and that it represents meaning.

Knowledge of research such as this reaffirms what perceptive teachers have already observed and encourages them to continue to examine their intuitions and to initiate innovative practices.

The term emergent literacy indicates a growing and developing use of written language interrelated with oral language as the child expands his role. Children who are moving towards literacy can be seen browsing in books, scribbling, pretending to read, writing lists and filling out forms. Some children use the typewriter or computer, some are fascinated with play money and cash registers. Learning centers, with their various themes and topics, allow children to stretch their learning experiences and experiment with materials new to them. There are many ways of becoming literate—children choose their own paths using the opportunities, challenges and material provided in their environments.

Expanding and Extending English

The curriculum of most early childhood programs is organized into themes that incorporate all subject areas. Classroom activities are integrated and concepts are connected within a broad framework or topic. This means that lessons don't occur in isolation and children are encouraged to find relationships and make connections. The encompassing framework is broad enough to allow for flexibility; confident teachers follow the lead of the children's expressed interests and directions while ensuring that both their overall goals and the bridge objectives for ESL children are met.

While individual teachers and groups of teachers have developed many excellent themes, these themes cannot be transplanted directly from one learning situation to another. Nevertheless, the ideas can be adopted, adapted and improved to fit children in different learning environments. Experimenting with different groups, collaborating with other teachers and parents, and continually assessing the program and evaluating children's progress will ensure positive results.

Most teachers can continue to use their current methods and organization, incorporating into them ways of extending the English-language facility of ESL children to help them reach their potential in all areas. Language is the window through which teachers can observe a child's way of thinking. Given help, young children make rapid progress in learning English once they are comfortable in the classroom and experience the need to use English to get things done. Their rapid growth in communication skills is exciting and rewarding for both the teacher and children.

It's worth keeping in mind, however, that Jim Cummins found that children learning English as a second language acquire a level of social fluency within about two years, but five to seven years is needed to develop the academic language needed to express abstract thought and to think critically. If we assume that, because they seem socially confident in the classroom, their English has developed to the level of their English-speaking peers, we do ESL children a disservice.

The following sample lesson, using William Toye's *The Loon's Necklace*, illustrates how ESL children can be helped to extend their use of English as they participate with their English-speaking counterparts in story time. Whether they are part of a small- or large-group activity, the techniques described can help them use English to think and to learn.

If the children are just beginning to learn English, they will need many visual aids to help them understand the story. Beforehand, take a few minutes with the ESL children to look at the pictures so that they can identify the loon, its necklace, the old man, the boy, the stream, the bear and the bow and arrow. A felt board and cutouts are useful because the children can come back to the board and use the cutouts again and again for reinforcement and for recreating the story themselves. As you read the story to the group, be sure to include the ESL children in the discussion by saying things like, "Show me the old man." Because this requires them only to point, it doesn't pressure them to respond orally before they're ready.

As their comprehension and confidence grow, however, encourage them to begin responding orally. For example, an exchange might go like this:

Teacher: Show me the old man.
ESL child (Pointing): There he is.

Questions that require only a yes or no answer don't require children to extend their use of language because they can respond with a gesture. On the other hand, teachers can ask questions designed to help ESL learners practice recognizing and using specific language patterns. These may include:

— Questions beginning with "who" or "what" that require an oral response to visual clues. Here's an example:
Teacher: Who is this?
Child: The old man.
Teacher: What's that?
Child: It's a bear.
— Questions asking "where" that help children express spatial concepts. For example:
Teacher: Where is the old man?
Child: In front of the tree.
— Questions asking "when" that help them express temporal relationships. For example:
Teacher: When did the boy see the old woman?
Child: After the old man shot the bear.
— Questions asking "why" are more difficult to answer because they require children to interpret information and call for more than surface comprehension of the story. Here's an example:
Teacher: Why did the old woman want the bear?
Child: Because she wanted to eat the meat.
— Questions asking "how" are the most difficult because they require children to interpret and reconstruct the content of the story. For example:
Teacher: How did the loon help the old man?
Child: He helped him see again *or* He dived under the water with the old man hanging onto his wings.

When they first arrive in a preschool or school, ESL children should be encouraged, but not required, to respond. When they are comfortable making one kind of response, encourage them to extend their language to include others. Keeping a journal of what they can use English for during the day helps teachers plan systematic extensions. The language children use is the language they know!

ESL children's skill at retelling, describing and comparing will reach the same level as their English-speaking peers slowly and steadily if they are encouraged and monitored. Parents can help by reading to their children in the home language and encouraging them to discuss not only stories but also what happened at school.

While comparing stories is a good way to help children learn about each other's cultures, the stories must be relevant to their interests and their level of comprehension. For example, a favorite story for most English-speaking children is *Little Red Riding Hood*, which could easily be worked into a forest theme. A Chinese version of this story, *Lon Po Po*, has been retold in English and is beautifully illustrated with pictures reminiscent of Chinese scroll painting.

Learning Centers

In most preschool and primary settings, learning centers, sometimes called activity centers or play areas, are used as an organizational structure for the classroom. These centers provide a variety of learning experiences and materials, encouraging children to explore, experiment, discover and socialize in their individual ways. As they do so, teachers can observe differences in learning styles as well as children's responses to stories, songs or field trips.

At first, some ESL children may be overwhelmed by the variety of new materials, the freedom to choose, which may be strange to them, and their inability to play as they would like to with other children because of a language barrier. Their responses may be quite different: some may withdraw silently, others may wander aimlessly from center to center, and still others may choose one area, such as the water table, and refuse to move. Sensitive teachers will be sympathetic to their need for time to adjust to the new environment.

Language cliques will form naturally as children from the same linguistic background are likely to play together using their home language. If the children's first language is to be respected, these groups cannot and should not be discouraged. At the same time, learning centers provide wonderful opportunities for teachers to encourage ESL children to extend their language by gradually encouraging friendships between ESL and non-ESL children.

Other groupings can also be organized, giving children of different cultures a chance to play together and use their common language—English. For example, the dramatic play area of one preschool class included a large fire truck, big enough for a child to sit on. There were also fire hats and toy hoses. This was a favorite play area for all the children, boys and girls. For ESL children, this became a catalyst for developing English and making new friends. The teacher took the opportunity to extend these new liaisons into other areas.

The number of learning centers in a classroom varies with the needs of the children, the imagination of the teacher and the limitations of the space. They are all useful for involving children in different activities, for extending language and thinking and for encouraging social interaction with different groups.

ESL children are part of the regular class and should be encouraged to participate with other children as much as possible. Learning centers give teachers a chance to observe ESL children closely as they interact with others, and to make note of their linguistic, cultural and social needs. If their English is to develop so that it can keep pace with their cognitive development, teachers need to ensure that the progression is logical and continuous, that language support is visual, aural and emotional and that stimulation is appropriate and consistent.

BLOCK CENTER

This area, like the others, provides opportunities for learning through play. It gives teachers a chance to observe the concepts ESL children have already developed in their first language, ensure that they have an opportunity to express these concepts in English, and plan for extension.

Number, order, shape, size, space and measurement are only a few of the concepts ESL children may have already developed in their first language. Age is not always a reliable measure of what children know: observing children as you interact with them is much more informative. For example, teachers might say things like, "This is a circle. Can you find a triangle?" "Let's put the triangle on top of the circle." "Where is the triangle? The circle?"

The possible extensions are endless, but they should be organized, not haphazard, so that ESL children are guided gradually towards expressing concepts appropriate to their stage of development. In addition to mathematical concepts, many other kinds of concepts can be introduced and extended during play in the block corner. For example, this center provides an ideal vehicle for integrating studies in various areas of the curriculum, such as science, social studies, literacy and mathematics.

ART OR CREATING CENTER

This area offers children the opportunity to create, experiment and respond personally to ideas or events. It is often a favorite choice of ESL children because it provides relief from trying to respond orally in English. The things children produce at this center provide insights into what they're thinking but cannot yet express in English. Discussing work-in-progress or completed work with the children gives teachers a chance to praise, invite appreciation from others and build their self-confidence.

Equipment at this center will include materials such as modeling dough, cookie cutters, paints, brushes, paper, coloring pens and pencils, fabric scraps, glue, easels and tables. Signing their art work reinforces the children's concept of one of the functions of written language—labeling.

DRAMATIC PLAY CENTER

Perhaps more than any other, this center provides both children and teachers with the best opportunities for learning. As children re-enact a story, role play in the house corner, choose costumes from the dress-up box or experiment with items from the prop box, they engage in many different cognitive activities: solving problems, hypothesizing, predicting and sequencing are but a few. Their dialogue with other children or a teacher helps them use language to clarify these thinking skills.

This center, popular with most children, is particularly appealing to ESL children. Here, they can become someone else, use English as another character and let their imaginations soar. Teachers watch and learn, participating only when required.

LIBRARY

In some early childhood education classrooms, the library is a center, a cozy, inviting corner where books are kept on shelves within easy reach of children who want to sit quietly to look and read. When children gather for circle or story time, this corner is often used. Although the library is located in a specific area, it is so integral to all the learning activities in some classrooms that children constantly carry books to other areas to use as references.

Whatever the design, the library is important for ESL children. They need to be encouraged to look at books, choose stories for reading, listen to tapes while following along in the books and borrow books to take home. They should also be encouraged to share books from home with other children. If the books are written in another language, it's a wonderful opportunity for the other children to see and learn about a different system of writing. The illustrations, too, may be very different from those in English books.

WRITING CENTER

Like the library, the writing center, too, is portable. Reading and writing are integral to language development and must be included in the activities of every classroom every day. Very young children learn to do things like write their names on their artwork, read the labels on classroom objects, manipulate the day, month and date on the calendar, choose the appropriate words to describe the weather, and recognize the month in which their birthdays occur.

ESL children should not be excluded from these activities. No matter how proficient they are in English when they enter the program, written representation should be part of their daily routine, because all four language modes—listening, speaking, writing and reading—are interrelated and develop concurrently.

SAND OR WATER TABLE

The presence of one of these centers doesn't preclude the presence of the other. We are treating them as one, however, because the activities they encourage are similar—only the medium is different. To conserve space, some teachers set up a sand table for a month or two, then switch to a water table. Equipment at both should include utensils for measuring, pouring, scooping and digging, and toys, such as cars, trucks, bulldozers, boats, balls, animals and people. Children discover for themselves that different-shaped containers may hold the same amount, that some objects float and others don't, that sand can be molded but water can't, and so on.

SCIENCE CENTER

The science center changes constantly to keep pace with the children's varying interests and the changing seasons of the year. Whether it's gathering colored leaves in the fall and observing what happens to them, looking at pictures of birds to help identify them when on a field trip, melting snow in winter, or planting seeds in the spring, the list of activities is endless. The purpose of the science center is to pique children's curiosity and encourage them to observe, question and draw conclusions. At this center, they learn to do things like make graphs and charts, record their observations and interpret data.

TABLE TOYS

This learning area often has a variety of toys and equipment, all of which need a flat surface for manipulation. They may include small cars and trucks, dolls or animals, puzzles and games, and scissors and paper for cutting out. Centers like this encourage the development of hand-eye coordination and fine motor skills, as well as providing a respite for ESL children who may want to play quietly on their own for a while.

MUSIC CENTER

The music center has a fascinating array of instruments that can be used to create different sounds and rhythms. They may be commercially created or homemade, whatever the teacher can provide—ukuleles, drums, marimbas, recorders, flutes, sticks, etc. Some centers have a record player or tape deck that may be used in large- or small-group activities.

The uses of the music center vary with every group. Sometimes, it's the focus for a singsong accompanied by a rhythm band, sometimes one or two children use it to listen quietly to a record or story on tape, or sometimes a child wants to play with one or more of the instruments, experimenting with ways of making different sounds.

Music is not usually confined to a specific area. Songs are used at transition times, at clean-up times, for group activities, and for saying goodbye. ESL children respond well to songs because it's often easier to sing something in another language than to say it.

. . . .

LANGUAGE AND LITERATURE
AS A WAY OF KNOWING

Who among us—no matter how old—doesn't love a story? "Tell me a story," "Read me a story," young children command their parents, and how wise they are, for stories are full of language in context. As children hear the same stories over and over again, the language—its music, vocabulary, structures and meaning—becomes part of their language repertoire.

Narrative and Story in Language Learning

For most young children, story time is magical. For a few moments, the impossible becomes possible and new characters people the world of their imaginations.

There are four elements to story time: the teller, the way of telling, the audience and the story. Each of these can be varied. The teller need not always be the teacher; she could be a parent or older child, a professional storyteller in person or on tape, or a child telling his own story. The way of telling may involve the teacher reading aloud or a tape recording of the teacher's or a professional's voice. Sometimes, stories are enhanced by dramatization. For example, the teacher may read the narrative while the children take the speaking parts. The audience may consist of one child, all the children or pairs of children reading to each other or telling stories. Sometimes the teacher is the audience. Finally, the variety of good stories for children is inexhaustible. They may be drawn from picture books, nursery rhymes, fairy tales, folktales, adventure stories, biographies, history, and stories by the children, their parents or other visitors.

By varying the stories, the teller can move the children back and forth between reality and fantasy. Concepts can be learned through stories and checked through dramatization. A dress-up box encourages make-believe based on stories. A good story well told can lead to other oral activities, such as discussion, drama, retelling, choral speaking or making up a similar story. While young ESL children should be encouraged to take part in all these activities, they should never be forced to participate. Some children need a longer listening period than others. They will talk when they're ready. Until then, teachers should ensure that they have lots of opportunities to hear language in context and make some meaning out of it.

When older children have learned enough English, they can be encouraged to tell stories in English that they originally learned in their home language. These may be both folktales and stories about themselves and their family. Teachers can make taking this risk more comfortable by using an encouraging tone of voice and gestures.

The literature of any culture is a precious part of its heritage. It's a record of human experience, past and present, that enables us to share the thoughts, feelings, joys and sorrows of other lives. It's important for all children to experience the world of literature as early as possible.

While stories are primarily for listening to, for enjoying, and for stimulating the imagination, they can be extended into almost every aspect of children's intellectual growth and development. Children learning a new language benefit from hearing stories, like Bill Martin Junior's *Brown Bear, Brown Bear*, that include a great deal of repetition and opportunities for substitution:

Brown Bear, Brown Bear, what do you see?
I see a black dog looking at me.
Black Dog, Black Dog, what do you see?
I see a _____ looking at me.

They need to hear stories that encourage them to chime in by, for example, chanting a chorus like this from *The Gingerbread Man*:

Run, run as fast as you can.
You can't catch me,
I'm the Gingerbread Man!

They need clear, uncluttered illustrations to help them clarify meaning and make connections between the spoken word and the representation. They also need to hear English versions of familiar stories from their own culture to help them draw on and make connections to their own previous experiences. *Lon Po Po*, a Chinese folktale that is a version of *Little Red Riding Hood*, is an example of a story like this.

Whether ESL children enter the system at the preschool or early primary level, these are essential first steps in becoming familiar with the patterns and music of the new language they're learning and with the structure and conventions of stories in English.

This, however, is not enough. With ESL children, as with their English-speaking counterparts, it's essential to encourage extensions of language and thought. This can't be neglected because the need to acquire the fundamentals of another language is so pressing. If ESL children are to have equal access to education, which is their right, then they must be taught the same skills as their English-speaking peers from the earliest levels of the educational system.

Teachers and other adults can use stories to encourage ESL children to ask and answer questions. These may be information questions—starting with "who," "what," "where" and "when"—or interpretive questions—starting with "why" and "how." The skills—categorizing, sequencing, predicting, connecting ideas and drawing conclusions—implicit in asking and answering these questions are essential to developing successfully the ability to think critically and evaluate.

At Home

An established body of evidence confirms the importance of reading to children at home in any language. For example, longitudinal studies conducted by Gordon Wells have demonstrated the significant positive relationship between reading at home and literacy development. Oral fluency, enjoyment of books and an eagerness to participate in learning are evident in children who are read to regularly at home.

The relationship described by Gordon Wells begins very early when a baby responds to the cadence and rhythm of an adult voice reading nursery rhymes and pointing out brightly colored illustrations. Interactive play, such as clapping hands together, jiggling a child on the knee and echoing exaggerated sounds, help make this experience happy and satisfying for both parent and child. Story time soon becomes a favorite, eagerly anticipated activity.

Toddlers enjoy stories about and pictures of physical activities they are struggling with themselves, such as using a spoon or putting on socks and shoes. Stories also help children anticipate and cope with the reality of important events, such as the arrival of a new sibling, a visit to the doctor or dentist and the first day at nursery school. Children at this stage also enjoy humor and delight in seeing how story characters cope with familiar situations. *How Do I Put It On?* by Shigeo Watanabe is an excellent example of a story like this.

Three- and four-year-olds have already internalized many social and linguistic conventions that, when violated, are rich in humor and provide them with a constant source of amusement. For example, when an adult asks, "What would you like for lunch?" a child may provoke hilarious laughter by responding, "Alligator pie." Catherine Garvey observed that as soon as children learn how something is supposed to be done, they have fun turning it upside down or distorting it in some way.

The sound of children's laughter sparked by humorous text or pictures represents more than amusement. It's also an indication of the their growing self-confidence and enjoyment.

The magic of folk and fairy tales helps children stretch their imaginations and develop their ability to play in a pretend world. It's very common to observe them weaving language, characters and events from the story world into everyday play activities. They're quite comfortable moving back and forth between the real world and the fantasy world, adjusting each to suit their purposes.

The following is an excerpt from the conversation of two four-year-olds negotiating their roles in preparation for pretend play. "Caught a glimpse" is a direct quotation from a story read to them.

First Child: You be the wolf. The wolf is hiding behind a tree. He caught a glimpse of Little Red Riding Hood.
Second Child: Okay. You put on the cape and I'll hide behind the tree.

Storybook reading at home is an interactive activity involving both parent and child. Both engage actively in constructing meaning as they ask and answer questions, discuss pictures and make predictions about the story together.

Children from homes where English is not spoken also have a rich story tradition. In some cultures, oral storytelling is still very much alive and children hear over and over again stories that have been passed from generation to generation. These stories are steeped in cultural tradition and values and become an important part of the children's developing knowledge of who they are and where they come from.

Many of the classical fairy tales have been translated or adapted into many languages. It's said, for example, that there are more than a hundred different versions of *Cinderella*. Of course, in the Punjab she doesn't have long golden hair!

Every culture has its own fairy tales, fables and folklore. Communicating this cultural heritage to children is an important part of the parents' role and is an integral part of a child's cognitive development. Parents and other significant adults are children's first teachers. Under their guidance, children develop their learning styles, social attitudes and oral fluency. Every child brings to the school a wealth of family tradition, cultural and social values, and linguistic knowledge. Whether this wealth is in the language used at school is irrelevant. When transfer to another language and culture is necessary, this is the base from which the transfer will take place.

At School

Early childhood is a period of tremendous growth, both physical and cognitive. The transition from home to school is the first big step into another learning environment. From a close one-on-one relationship with the "knower" at home, the child must now move into a relationship that involves sharing the "knower" with several children. Every child enters school equipped with her own learning style, her own expectations of school and the teacher, and her own unique way of negotiating meaning.

Although good early childhood programs encourage growth in all aspects of a child's development (social, emotional, aesthetic, physical, intellectual and linguistic), learning is facilitated when children can apply their own experience and background knowledge to the task at hand. "Start where the child is" is a maxim that holds as true today as it did in the past.

Sharing stories, especially familiar ones, makes an ideal bridge into the new learning environment. However, for a child who has always experienced story time one-on-one or for one who is unfamiliar with English, circle time with the whole group may be intimidating at first. Volunteers chosen from the parent group or older children can help provide a transition period by reading to children in small groups.

No matter what the setting of children's initial reading or storytelling experiences, there are many ways to encourage them to respond to and share stories—using felt boards or puppets and dressing up are only a few of these. When children share their responses to and representations of a story, they learn from each other. Their responses become a stepping stone to further development. This means that every response, no matter how unusual, deserves acceptance and respect. If their responses are treated this way, children will gradually become comfortable, trusting, open, and eager to explore, discover and wonder.

The way children expand and extend the new information they receive depends on the opportunities, stimulation and encouragement received from adults and the learning environment.

Some teachers use a literature-based curriculum to encourage exploration by extending chosen themes into learning center activities. The children's responses to the stories indicate the direction in which the theme can develop—through artwork or at the dramatic play or science center, the block corner, the math table and the writing center. Activities at any and all of these centers can elicit responses that the children will expand on and extend themselves if they feel safe. Using the children's responses as a guide when planning activities helps them feel ownership and encourages them to take responsibility for their own learning.

This kind of interactive teaching is not always easy. For some teachers, it is very natural; for others, it is uncomfortable and unnerving because of its unpredictability. It is still the teacher's responsibility to guide learning towards the goals set out in the curriculum. The challenge is to guide the children's initiatives so that these goals are achieved.

Teachers who use a literature-based approach report that, initially, there is a great deal of discussion, research and study. Some themes, such as The Forest, Journeys, No Place like Home and Memories, work well; others don't. Finding appropriate stories and related books is time-consuming. Adhering to the tenets of early childhood education by maintaining a sensitive, responsive approach is demanding. But it does get easier with experience and the rewards—children whose ideas tumble out, whose activities abound with innovative suggestions, and whose exuberance reflects an eagerness to learn—are worth the extra effort. Teachers interested in finding out more about these ideas might begin by reading *Storyworlds*, another book in the Pippin Teachers' Library (see the chapter titled "Resources.")

Across Cultures

In most school communities in the 1990s, young children who don't speak English are integrated into regular preschool or primary classes. The theory underlying this practice is that young children are capable of accommodating the patterns of an additional language more readily than older learners because their ability to use their first or native language has not yet developed fully.

Unfortunately, this theory is sometimes interpreted too simplistically. Some people, even educators, think that young children simply "pick up" another language, as they would the measles, and that no intervention is necessary. On the contrary, young ESL learners need teachers who are attuned to the similarities and differences between first and second language acquisition, are aware of cross-cultural practices and beliefs in child-rearing, and sensitive to the importance of cultural and linguistic identity in developing and maintaining self-esteem.

Administrators who warmly welcome ESL children and their families into their schools and recognize their need for extra language experience and support make a tremendous difference for everyone. They initiate the creation of a healthy multicultural environment that benefits all children and helps them prepare for the global community in which they will live their lives. We know of one principal who learned how to say "hello" or "good morning" in the various languages represented in her school. As she walked down the corridor, she greeted every child in his or her own language and was rewarded with a delighted smile.

The literature of any culture provides windows through which readers can experience, however vicariously, different ways of thinking and living. Multicultural literature is a term that has appeared frequently in educational journals in the past few years. It's important for teachers and parents not only to have a clear idea of what this term encompasses for the children in their care but also to be capable of evaluating carefully the great variety of books listed under this rubric. Children develop an awareness of cultural and physical characteristics at a very young age. Guidance at this stage can foster positive attitudes and prevent the formation of stereotypical concepts. The following are suggestions various teachers have used to help choose books for young children.

— Examine both content and illustrations for stereotypes and avoid them.
— Choose books that reflect the pluralistic global society that is familiar to the children and relevant to their daily lives.
— Choose books that encourage the children to learn about the heritages of their classmates.
— Choose stories that are authentic. Check that the author has more than a passing acquaintance with the story's culture. Check the illustrations, too; although they may be artistically pleasing, they may not relate to the story or be relevant for the children.
— Help the children celebrate the similarities among all people and delight in the differences that make the world we live in bright and interesting. Everyone shares in feeling happiness and sadness, love and hate, kindness and cruelty, and justice and injustice. But not ev-

eryone shares the same experiences and celebrations, the same food or eating utensils, the same kinds of living quarters, the same music, or the same games.

— Choose books that are realistic. In the world in which these children are growing up, there is discrimination and bias. But even very young children can learn to respect the rights of others, which is the basis for developing an appreciation of human rights in society.

— Above all, choose books that appeal to children. Stories are primarily for listening to, for enjoying, for sparking the imagination and for sharing.

Many folktales and fairy tales from other languages and cultures have been translated or retold. When teachers can find a story familiar to children in their home language, it helps build the crucial bridge between the known and the unknown and exposes the other children to stories from different cultures.

Earlier in this chapter, the importance of reading at home was discussed. Parents of ESL children may not have access to many books from their home country because it may have been very difficult to bring books with them when they emigrated. Teachers who realize that part of all children's individuality is rooted in their racial, cultural and religious heritage are constantly challenged to find links between home and school.

When a teacher urges parents to read to their children, immigrant parents often think this means reading in English. They need to know that it's important for children to continue developing, both linguistically and cognitively, in their first language. To facilitate this, teachers need to encourage parents to continue reading and discussing stories in the home language.

Some teachers use home visits to promote the importance of enjoying books at home. Armed with one or more books especially chosen for an individual child, a teacher arrives for the scheduled visit. Part of the time is spent reading or looking at the book, with the child cuddled close to the teacher. The parent or caregiver sees the teacher modeling reading to the child while the child enjoys the individual attention of the teacher. Subsequently, the teacher may observe that the book chosen for the reading session at home has become the child's favorite choice during classroom reading time.

Other teachers invite parents into the classroom to observe or participate in reading or telling stories. Sometimes parents can be consulted about a story from their culture that has been retold in English.

Libraries and librarians play an important role in fostering interest and enthusiasm for multicultural literature among families new to the country. Many libraries, both school and public, now have a growing selection of children's books in many languages. Story hours, usually held once a week, at which both parents and children are always welcome, offer a wealth of opportunity for listening and sharing and later borrowing books to take home.

It is ultimately the teacher, however, who is responsible for coordinating efforts and providing the motivation for the out-of-school reading activities that are so crucial to children's cognitive and emotional development.

Examples of children's stories from many cultures are found in the chapter titled "Resources."

. . . .

BUILDING BRIDGES

Nowadays, children aged three to seven who are learning English as a second language are usually integrated with other children their own age, both English- and non-English-speaking. Developmentally, they are probably on a par with their peers, but this development has taken place in another language and culture. All children differ in age, motor skills, reasoning skills and knowledge of facts and how things work. ESL children also differ in their behavior patterns, their competency in English, and their learning styles. This means that children with a wide range of needs, skills and abilities may be found in a single preschool or primary class.

Building Bridges to the Mainstream

ESL children may be ahead of their peers in some areas of the curriculum and behind in others. To help pinpoint the best program for individual ESL children, teachers can ask the following questions. The first three apply to all children. The answers help establish where each child is and set the direction of his program. The final three are particularly important for ESL children because the answers help identify areas where extra language support may be needed.

— What should a child of this age know or be able to do according to curriculum and development guidelines?
— What is this child's learning style?

— What is this child's current level of concept development, reasoning skills, manipulative skills and social behavior?
— What linguistic knowledge, concepts, reasoning skills, manipulative skills and social behavior does this child need to be able to function comfortably with the peer group?
— What is this child's current level of English?
— How can this child be helped to gain control of the language, learning style, concepts, reasoning skills, manipulative skills and social behavior that will enable her to function comfortably with her peers and reach her potential as a student?

ASSESSMENT

In large urban centers, school districts often have reception centers for ESL children and their families. Although it is not usual to assess very young children formally, they and their families are carefully interviewed and parents are given both written and oral information, in their own language if necessary, about programs and expectations.

If there is no reception center in your area, the classroom teacher and an ESL resource teacher, if there is one, can conduct an assessment by observing the child over a period of days and weeks. In addition, information obtained from the parents at the time of registration may prove helpful.

If standardized tests are administered, do not place your trust in them; they are culture-bound, the language used may be too sophisticated, and the children may not be used to taking tests and may not present their best work. Regardless of how well or poorly children do on a test, they should be placed with their peers, even if there is evidence of slow linguistic or cognitive development. Programs for these children should be developed in consultation with specialists.

BRIDGE ACTIVITIES

Because it takes five to seven years for ESL children to master English at the same level as their native English-speaking peers, they will be continually building bridges between cultures and languages. Early childhood practices are important for all children. However, the responses of ESL children should be monitored carefully so that teachers can provide additional stimulation as necessary. For example, questions like the following about the calendar might be put to all the children every day:

Teacher: What day is today?
Children: It's Monday.
Teacher: What will tomorrow be?
Children: Tomorrow will be Tuesday.

When they participate in this activity, ESL children learn both the question and the answer. The first question introduces the present tense of the verb "to be" and the question form "what?" The second question introduces the future tense of "to be." The names of the days of the week are learned in context.

The teacher can provide an ESL child with extra stimulation and reinforcement by asking him to point to Monday on the calendar. Because he's asked to point, no oral response is necessary. His action will indicate whether he understands.

If the teacher suggests that all the children join in saying— or singing—the names of the days of the week, ESL children have an opportunity to practice without being conspicuous.

There are many ways to organize activities, such as counting, so that ESL children have ample opportunity to practice without being singled out to answer orally on their own. The following scenarios illustrate a couple of techniques:

Teacher: What's the date today?
Children: It's September 21.
Teacher: Let's count all the days up to today. (As the teacher points to the numbers on the calendar, the children respond chorally. Again, the ESL child has an opportunity to practice numbers inconspicuously.)

Teacher: Let's count all the boys (or girls) in the room. Baljeet, touch each child as we count. (Baljeet can hear the numbers, but is not required to provide an individual response. She can participate orally when she's ready.)

The teacher might also suggest that ESL children teach the other children to count from one to ten in their home language. All children enjoy experimenting with the different sounds and this activity gives the ESL children the chance to be the knowers.

Throughout the day, ESL children need encouragement and stimulation to engage in activities that will require them to use English to accomplish what they want to do. Remember, the language they learn is the language they use.

VARIATIONS IN LEARNING STYLES

It cannot be said too often that learning styles vary from culture to culture and, indeed, even within cultures. Some children are taught to watch and learn or to experiment by themselves and then perform. Other children are taught to listen quietly, absorb and participate in group responses. In many North American families, young children are encouraged to learn by discovery, trial and error and by individual participation accompanied by continual linguistic exchange.

In some cultures, teachers are regarded with a respect approaching awe. Children use only the honorific "teacher" to address them. Because they represent authority, children don't look at them directly when speaking to them; instructions are listened to in silence and are not questioned. In the new school, however, the friendly, informal person who plays games with the children, who sits on the floor and tells stories in a warm, cozy atmosphere may take some getting used to—by both parents and children. Some children maintain complete silence, sometimes in both languages, until they feel comfortable in the strange surroundings. This silence should not be misunderstood; it is probably the silence of stress rather than a silence that indicates inherent difficulties in learning.

Some children come from illiterate families. Neither they nor their parents nor grandparents have ever attended school. As a result, the family may have no expectations of school and no real understanding of what education means. Children from families like this often evince inappropriate social behavior at school, exacerbated by a total lack of comprehension of what a written code is. This is quite different from the situation with preliterate children, those who have not yet learned to read. Because they come from literate homes, preliterate children have a concept of written language; they've seen their parents and other adults reading and writing;

they're familiar with books and have been exposed to written symbols that they know have meaning.

The entry point for ESL children from illiterate families is quite different from that of other ESL children. These children need much more time to adjust to oral English and go through the long, slow process of realizing that written symbols can also have meaning. As migration patterns change, teachers may meet more and more families that have never experienced written language. They present a whole new challenge that requires innovative approaches and infinite patience.

In many cases, families have been forced to flee their homes because of political disruption and war. They may have been forced to live a hand-to-mouth existence as refugees, or they may have been cramped together in camps, waiting for acceptance into a welcoming country. In cases like this, the flow of information children normally absorb in the course of daily living has been interrupted. These children may have no concept of regular meals, only food; of bedtime, only sleep; of family, only people; of play, only fear. Teachers can only guess at their lack of ordinary childhood experiences and at the trauma that may have impeded normal development. The period of adjustment for these children may be long and their acquisition of English may be slow. The teacher's most important role may be to provide a safe, stable environment for the child and encouragement for his family until everyone feels comfortable and ready to learn.

Building Bridges to the Home

Like most parents the world over, parents of ESL children want the best for their children. In most cases, they will have had experiences with schools in their homeland and these will form the backdrop against which they will judge the educational system in their adopted land. They may or may not have had experiences with preschool education, but they certainly will have some expectations and concerns.

Some arrive with high expectations of what the school system can do for their child; some with high expectations of what their child can achieve. When these expectations are unrealistic, regular parent-teacher conferences may be helpful. If the teacher explains the process and nature of second language learning, the parents will, over time, develop more reasonable expectations of the individual child.

Some parents may be going through personal trauma as they find it difficult to get or perhaps hold a job that may be far below what they are trained for and capable of doing. Some mothers may be obliged to enter the work force for the first time and may feel the strain of working outside the home while caring for a young family. The family's support systems may have disappeared and adjustments may lead to distress and confusion.

In most classrooms of the 1990s, young ESL children are integrated with their peer groups. However, some parents may be surprised to find that their child's class includes children from six or seven linguistic groups in addition to the English-speaking children. Teachers may be called upon to help parents come to grips with the multicultural makeup of the classroom and the surrounding community. This can be accomplished gradually by making sure that parents of different cultures serve together on committees and work as helpers on field trips and volunteers in the classroom.

Teachers who show that they care about the ESL children and their families and are ready to help them as they settle in to a new way of life, learn a new language and become used to a new culture will be remembered long after the children have left the school. If possible, teachers should talk to all parents about the center or school before the children attend for the first time. If parents are given an indication of some of the activities the children will engage in, particularly those youngsters are likely to enjoy, they can help prepare them for this new experience in the home language. They can also reassure the children that they will return at a particular time to take them home.

All parents should be encouraged to observe the class in action so they can watch the routines and procedures and see how their child fits in. Teachers who create a welcoming climate in their classrooms will be rewarded by cooperative parents and self-assured children.

If some parents seem reluctant to take part, this should not be interpreted as a lack of interest or caring. There may be a variety of reasons for this apparent reluctance, none of which have anything to do with a lack of interest in their children. Perhaps both parents are working and are not available during school hours; perhaps they had an unhappy experience at school when they were young; perhaps they're embarrassed by their own lack of education. ESL parents may experience the same anxieties, and these may be exacerbated by their unfamiliarity with both the language and the school system.

ESL parents should also be told what they can do at home to assist children in both language learning and concept development. This may include things like taking the children to places where English is spoken and encouraging older children to read to younger children in both English and their home language.

The following are some activities that will involve all parents in their children's education and encourage positive attitudes towards people from other cultures:

— For the first few days, encourage caregivers to stay in the classroom for a little while and, on leaving, to explain to the child that they will be returning soon.

— Suggest that the child bring a favorite toy or object to class as security during the initial settling in period.

— Recruit parents as volunteers to help with some of the daily routines. In this way, they will learn the center or classroom procedures.

— Seek parents' help when making materials needed for games or for particular learning activities. This may be ideal for working parents because they don't necessarily need to do this in the classroom.

— Suggest to some parents that volunteering in the classroom or center will help them improve their English.

— Children enjoy hearing what life was like in the "olden days." Some parents may enjoy sharing memories of their childhood in another country and culture.

— Children also enjoy learning about and tasting different foods. Parents might be asked to bring a favorite recipe to the group and help prepare it with the class. Shopping for the ingredients provides an opportunity for children to learn more about the stores in their community.

— Invite parents from different backgrounds to sing or dance for the children or to show ethnic costumes.

— Invite families to an open house, a meet-the-teacher night or a lunch that the children have helped plan.

- If parents from one culture are entertaining the children, ask parents from other cultures to be part of the audience.
- Set up a discussion group of a few parents (ESL and non-ESL) to help the newcomers to the country understand the educational system and share ideas about child-rearing practices.
- If possible, have bulletins or letters translated for ESL parents to ensure that they understand the contents.
- Take both English-speaking and non-English-speaking parents with you on field trips.
- Invite parents to view slides of their children involved in activities at the center.
- Hold an intercultural pot luck lunch or dinner and invite families to share a dish associated with their cultural background.
- Ensure that all adults working in the ESL preschool program are aware of the range of cultural home environments with regard to discipline, general behavior patterns and the degree of personal freedom the children have experienced.

INTERPRETERS

If parents are to be involved in their children's education and in class and school activities, it may be necessary to provide an interpreter. It's important for teachers and parents to have opportunities to talk face-to-face, either directly or through an interpreter. The interpreter may be a family member or friend who is fairly fluent in both English and the parents' language. Ethnic groups and social service organizations sometimes have resource lists of volunteer interpreters and some school districts employ multicultural workers.

GOALS OF THE PROGRAM

Parents will want to know what the goals of the program are—what they can expect their children to achieve in both the short and long terms.

The goals of the program might include the following:

- To help children develop and maintain a sense of self-worth.

— To help children develop and preserve pride in their heritage.
— To help ESL children become increasingly proficient in English.
— To help children learn about each other's cultures.
— To help children become comfortable with diversity.

Parents tend to have very high expectations of their children. In many cases, they have left their own country so that their children will have an opportunity to get a better education that will, in turn, lead to better employment prospects. Teachers can help parents develop realistic expectations by explaining that it takes time—five to seven years—for a child to master a new language and by discussing the child's progress with the parents at regular intervals. Parents should be encouraged to ask questions.

Some parents will be unhappy with some of the practices in English-medium schools; for example, the discipline may appear lax as children wander from table to table talking to each other. They may believe that spending time at the sand table contributes little to the child's education and expect the focus to be on reading, writing and mathematics. At parent meetings, some teachers invite parents to participate in examples of the children's activities, then lead a discussion about what—and how—children learn from them. This is particularly helpful for ESL parents who may be unfamiliar with urban classrooms.

Building Bridges to the Community

For a community to be aware of the diversity in the student population in its midst and its responsibility towards them, teachers should be aware of—and prepared to foster—the relationships that exist among schools, preschools, day care centers and the surrounding communities. Three types of communities affect schools:

— Geo-political communities—groups that are limited by fixed physical boundaries; that is, neighborhoods, reservations and ghettos; school districts; electoral districts; municipalities, provinces and states; nations. A hierarchy may exist among these communities. For example, municipalities, provinces and states may be able to impose their will on school districts.

— Common-interest communities—groups of people that share a common history, language or culture, or religious or political ideology. These may include families, speech communities having a common language or dialect, minority groups defined either by ethnicity or socio-economic status, and ideological groups, such as political or religious groups or pressure groups concerned about a single issue.

— Professional groups—groups that are directly concerned with some aspect of child care and education, including second language teaching. These may include parents' or teachers' associations, public health nurses, and speech and language pathologists.

These communities may affect preschool programs, kindergartens and schools in three ways. First, communities can provide resources, financial, material and human, for the various programs. Second, they can benefit from programs that, by providing children with a good start in life, help ensure that, as adults, they will make significant contributions to society. Third, communities can, through the various policies they initiate, control the goals, size, continuity and quality of programs.

It is therefore important for preschool and school teachers on the one hand and the various communities on the other hand to recognize the relationships that exist between them, and to use these relationships solely for the good of the children. Let's look at communities and teachers separately, considering the kinds of actions that are possible and beneficial for both.

COMMUNITIES

Communities are made up of people who differ from each other in knowledge, experiences, attitudes, beliefs and prejudices. For communities to react positively to the needs of young ESL children, they must know what these needs are and what kinds of resources would best meet these needs. Most communities are probably capable of providing the following resources:

72

— *Funds*: Preschool programs need money to rent suitable accommodation, pay staff salaries and purchase materials. This money may be raised by charging fees or receiving government grants or a combination of the two. Funding for kindergarten and the primary grades is part of the education budget. What must never be forgotten is the importance of giving all children, ESL and non-ESL, a good start in their early years. If the needs of young children are neglected, society will pay many times over in later years.

— *People*: Individuals of different ages and backgrounds can act as teacher aides or as resources, supplying information on topics of concern and interest to both children and teachers. These topics may include health and recreation or cultural activities like songs and games.

— *Materials*: Community groups and commercial enterprises often supply pamphlets, films, posters and pictures free of charge. These can supplement what is supplied by the educational institution, whether it's a day care center, preschool or school.

— *Field Trips*: Children learn far more from seeing and experiencing for themselves various aspects of the world beyond the classroom than from being simply told about them. Hence, field trips to, for example, museums, art galleries, local stores or a community center increase children's vocabulary and overall fluency as they ask questions about and comment on what they see, while simultaneously enabling them to learn new concepts and expand on their previous knowledge.

TEACHERS AND COMMUNITY

We've already commented on the role of the community as a classroom resource and the need for parental involvement. At the same time, the school can also become a resource for the community by opening the door of opportunity in education for children and their families. A community may consist of diverse groups and individuals with many voices. The school can often reach out and communicate effectively with all these groups and individuals. The classroom teacher is the catalyst who makes things happen by initiating activities like the following:

— Taking a group of children to visit a nursing home to sing, perform and tell stories.
— Encouraging children to write thank-you letters to places they've visited or letters to the editor of the community newspaper.
— Taking children shopping in local stores to buy classroom supplies.
— Taking children to the community library on a regular basis.

These trips are more than entertaining outings. Teachers carefully plan pre- and post-trip activities so that the children gradually learn about the makeup of their community.

Building Bridges to Other Teachers

Most children in developed countries today have had some kind of preschool experience outside the home. Because kindergartens have been part of the school system for many years, children under the age of five often attend a day care center, a play school run by parents, or a preschool with qualified teachers. Whatever the venue, the preschool experience the child brings to the kindergarten classroom is very important.

Early childhood educators can take some positive steps towards building professional cooperation by encouraging open-door policies in all the classrooms in their community. Joint projects involving preschool and kindergarten classes, teacher exchanges or visits, and regular ECE and parent meetings featuring discussions on all kinds of issues relevant to the community are some of the ways this can be achieved. Within the school, teachers should schedule time to talk to each other. For example:

— The kindergarten teacher can help the child make the transition from preschool experiences to "formal" education.
— The kindergarten teacher can often offer insights into or solutions to a problem a child may be having in her first or second year of primary education.

— A grade 3 teacher may be able to learn a great deal about how a child solves a problem from his previous teachers.
— The librarian is a resource whom most teachers treasure. Her involvement is invaluable in planning, suggesting resources and expanding classroom possibilities.
— Teachers can visit each other's classrooms.
— Teachers can plan joint projects or themes.

The years between three and seven are a time of wondrous growth and development. Children expand their world, their language and their ideas. They set a pattern for learning, for cooperating with others and for living productively. Whatever the children's linguistic or cultural background, it is the responsibility of all adults who have contact with them at home, at school and in the community to give them as much help and support as they need. They are the hope of the world.

POOLING RESOURCES

"Adopt and adapt and improve," the saying goes. Some of the most effective teachers are those who are open to using resources from agencies and commercial enterprises that are often readily available to preschool and school teachers. Here are some suggestions for organizing the pooling of resources:

— Build a network in the district of all the people interested in any aspect of early childhood education. Meet regularly with plenty of time for coffee and chat.
— Create a center where people can deposit materials and write ideas on large cards. Build in a system for borrowing the materials.
— Build up a central lending library of teacher references containing both books and journals. (See the chapter titled "Resources" for suggestions to help start things off.)
— Create a package of learning materials on different topics suitable for children of different ages with different levels of fluency in English.
— Write or telephone commercial enterprises that might have giveaways such as brochures, cardboard figures, small booklets, pictures, posters, etc. Prepare a list of

cooperating companies. Give someone the responsibility for keeping the list up-to-date.

— Develop—and share—ideas for learning centers.
— Build a list of public places (e.g., the fire hall, post office, art gallery, community center) and commercial operations (e.g., a dairy or supermarket) where groups of young children are welcome to walk around and talk about what they see.
— Provide opportunities for teachers to observe other teachers in similar situations.
— Provide opportunities for social workers, administrators and others to meet with teachers or to be welcome visitors to a classroom.
— Invite college instructors and university professors with an interest in early childhood education to a meeting to see what resources they can offer.
— Find resource people in the community who will assist with the children by teaching a song or a game or by bringing in an interesting artifact. Make a list of these people for the resource center.
— Establish a protocol for using volunteer aides.

Building Bridges to Tomorrow

The common goal that day care centers, schools, school districts, municipalities, states, provinces and nations must work toward is a language policy for children that citizens can accept and work with. The language policy would make statements about teaching English as a second language, about maintaining ESL children's first language and about bilingualism.

In addition to clarifying the language rights of children, the language policy would also provide answers for questions like, Do ESL children have a right to be taught English? To maintain their home language? To bilingual education?

This statement of children's rights should be preceded by a statement of philosophy. This might say, for example, "The philosophy of the language policy is that all students, regardless of linguistic and cultural background, will have the opportunity to develop their potential to the fullest."

Within the framework of a language policy containing statements of philosophy and rights, schools and school districts can then proceed to formulate goals for their programs that are in accord with the policy. Some of these were suggested on page 70.

When formulating goals, the following issues need to be taken into account:

— *Funding*: How much money is available and from whom?
— *Teacher training*: What should teachers know and who will teach it to them?
— *Programs*: What kind of program will suit particular situations?
— *Curriculum*: What should be stressed in the curriculum? Language? Culture? Subject matter?
— *Methodology*: How should the curriculum be taught?
— *Accountability*: To whom should those administering and working within the program be accountable?
— *Research*: What research is needed to help improve the program and who should do it?
— *Parental involvement*: How can parents be involved in the program?
— *Cultural diversity*: How can centers and schools work with communities so that cultural diversity is recognized and appreciated?
— *Evaluation*: What aspects of the program should be evaluated and by whom? Who should receive the report? How should suggested improvements be implemented?

When caring for young children, whether they're English- or non-English-speaking, the words of Alexander Israel Wittenberg are worth remembering:

"The privileged child comes to school wanting and expecting to learn, and he will have many standards and experiences outside of school to complement and, if necessary, supplement the experience of learning that the school creates. To the less fortunate child, education is what his school does. If it does too little, or if it does the wrong thing, it will strike at the very roots of the entire future education of that child.

"Very high priority must be given to early education. We lay the very foundation for educational democracy, and for equality of educational opportunity, if we see to it that every child, and particularly the least fortunate, begins his education under the best conditions possible."

. . . .

APPENDIX A — LANGUAGE

Languages consist of five systems: phonology, morphology, syntax, semantics and pragmatics. While a brief overview of these systems follows, those who wish to learn more about how language works will find useful references in the following chapter under the heading, Language and Grammar.

Language—A System of Systems

PHONOLOGY

Phonology is the study of speech sounds.

A phoneme is the smallest speech sound that makes a difference in meaning. For example, /t/ and /d/ are phonemes because "ten" and "den" have different meanings determined by the initial sound of each word. The symbols for phonemes are written between slashes to distinguish them from letters. Not all English phonemes are found in other languages. ESL children must learn a new sound system when they learn English.

The International Phonetic Alphabet is a symbol system used to represent the sounds made by the consonants and vowels of English. Most dictionaries indicate pronunciation by using IPA symbols. There are twenty-four consonant phonemes and about fifteen vowel phonemes in English, all represented by the twenty-six letters of the alphabet. The number of vowel phonemes varies according to the dialect of the speaker. For example, a Scot, a Newfoundlander and an Alabaman will probably sound very different when reading the same sentence because of variations in the vowel phonemes—and intonation patterns—they use when speaking.

The following IPA symbols represent the twenty-four consonant phonemes of English:

/p/	pin	/s/	sip
/b/	bin	/z/	zip
/t/	tin	/ʃ/	ship
/d/	din	/ʒ/	vision
/k/	kill	/m/	mine
/g/	gill	/n/	nine
/tʃ/	chill	/ŋ/	king
/dʒ/	Jill	/w/	will
/f/	fine	/h/	hill
/v/	vine	/j/	yet
/θ/	thigh	/l/	Lil
/ð/	thy	/r/	rill

And these are the IPA symbols representing the fifteen most frequently used vowel phonemes:

Front Vowels		Back Vowels	
/i/	beat	/ɑ/	bought
/ɪ/	bit	/ɔ/	law
/eɪ/	bait	/əʊ/	boat
/ɛ/	bet	/ʊ/	pull
/æ/	bat	/u/	pool

Central Vowels		Diphthongs	
/ə/	sofa	/aʊ/	bough
/ʌ/	butt	/aɪ/	buy

Intonation refers to variations in pitch. In English, statements and questions beginning with "who," "when," "where," "why" and "how" start on a steady pitch, but rise and fall at the end of the utterance. Questions beginning with an auxiliary verb (e.g., Is Bob happy?) begin on a steady pitch and end on a rising pitch.

Morphology is the study of the structure of words.

Morphemes are the smallest *meaningful* elements into which words can be broken down. For example, "uninteresting" can be broken down into three morphemes—"un" (a prefix signaling a negative), "interest" (the root word) and "ing" (a suffix that has a number of functions in English but, in this case, signals that the word is a an adjective). "Uninteresting" can also be broken down into five syllables—un-in-ter-est-ing. Unlike morphemes, which are meaningful elements, syllables often have no meaning.

SYNTAX

Syntax is the study of the arrangement of words in sentences to express meaning.

As a rule, basic sentences in English follow a Subject-Verb-Object (S-V-O) pattern.

SEMANTICS

Semantics is the study of meaning in language.

The meaning assigned to a particular word is the result of consensus by a group of speakers; for example, a table is called a table not because of any inherent qualities it possesses but because English speakers have agreed to give it this label. Past experiences combine with the current context to play a part in defining meaning.

PRAGMATICS

Pragmatics is the study of the factors influencing our choice of language. It has to do with what we say, when we say it and why we say it.

"Communicative competence" describes our ability to use language appropriately in social contexts while "linguistic competence" refers to our ability to use it grammatically correctly.

. . . .

RESOURCES

The teacher is, in our opinion, the most important person in the educational system, and the teacher of young children is the most important teacher of all. To be maximally effective, the teacher needs good backup services. Sometimes these are available, but not everyone is aware of them: sometimes they are not available and ought to be. The following support services are among the most important:

— Teacher reference library.
— An ESL consultant or experienced teacher who can visit the center or classroom.
— Teacher aides.
— Alternative sets of commercial ESL materials and games (perhaps obtainable on loan).
— Audio-visual aids and the necessary hardware.
— A bilingual home-school worker
— Testing services.
— Buddies.
— Workshops and in-service training
— A dress-up box.
— Other teachers—e.g., librarian, music teacher, art teacher.

In addition, the classroom should be well-supplied with enough furniture, materials and educational toys to enable the teacher to run a varied and flexible program.

Community Resources

These fall into a variety of categories as follows:

— *Materials:* Posters, advertising materials, catalogues, travel folders, carpet ends, scrap material (cloth and wood), cardboard tubes, plastic bottles, empty spools, clothes for the dress-up box.
— *People*: Volunteer aides of all ages, professional resource people such as a police officer, fire fighter, public health nurse, dental hygienist, ethnic groups, musical groups.
— *Places*: Local stores, hospital, fire hall, police station, nursing home, bakery, factory, restaurant, bus station, railway station, harbor, garden centers.
— *Recreational facilities*: Community centers, skating rinks, parks, aquarium, museum, art gallery, concert.

Children's Books

AFRICA

Appiah, Sonia. *Amoko and the Efua Bear.* Illustrated by Carol Easman. New York: Macmillan, 1988.

Amoko, a five-year-old girl who lives in Ghana, takes her favorite teddy bear, called Efua, with her everywhere. One day, she leaves him outside and he is lost. Efua has adventures of his own before he and Amoko are reunited. Colorful full-page illustrations help children relate to situations that are familiar although they are set in a different country.

Mollel, Tololwa M. *The King and the Tortoise.* Illustrated by Kathy Blankey. Toronto: Lester Publishing, 1993.

A traditional story from Cameroon, this delightful tale has counterparts in many cultures. Who is the cleverest—the hare, the fox, the elephant or the tortoise? The King has offered an unusual challenge to find out. The illustrations enhance the story and the setting.

Yolen, Jane. *The Emperor and the Kite*. Illustrated by Ed Young. New York: Philomel Books, 1988.

When the emperor is imprisoned in a high tower, it is his youngest and smallest daughter whom he has always ignored in favor of her brothers and sisters who rescues him with her kite. The beautiful illustrations are based on Oriental papercut technique.

Yacowitz, Caryn. *The Jade Stone*. Illustrated by Ju-Hong Chen. New York: Holiday House, 1992.

A Chinese folktale adapted for English-speaking children is accompanied by illustrations so vivid they tell the story by themselves. When the Great Emperor of All China orders Chanlo to carve him a dragon of wind and fire from a piece of perfect jade, Chanlo discovers that the stone has other ideas. The story carries a gentle message about artistic truth.

Louie, Ai-Ling. *Yeh-Shen: A Cinderella Story from China*. Illustrated by Ed Young. New York: Philomel Books, 1982.

This classic Chinese tale dates from the T'ang Dynasty (618-907 A.D.). The oldest European version was found in Italy dated 1634. This story, familiar in all cultures, can be enjoyed by children of all ages. A good opportunity to compare and contrast plots, details and settings.

Young, E. *Lon Po Po: A Red Riding Hood Story from China*. New York: Philomel Books, 1989.

Three young children who are left on their own manage to outwit the wicked wolf.

Marshak, Samuel. Translated from Russian by Thomas P. Whitney. *The Months Brothers*. Illustrated by Diane Stanley. New York: William Morrow, 1983.

A Slavic folktale set in Bohemia, this is the story of a young girl who outwits her greedy stepmother and stepsister with the help of the 12 Months Brothers.

Tharlet, E. Translated and adapted by Anthea Bell from *The Brothers Grimm*. *Jack in Luck*. Saxonville, Massachusetts: Petra Book Studio, 1992.

Jack is one of those delightfully simple folklore characters who is duped by everyone he meets. Recall "Simple Simon" and *Jack and the Beanstalk*. This Jack works seven years for a lump of gold, then sets out to carry it home to his old mother. Because it is a heavy burden, he trades it for something lighter. After a succession of disastrous trades, he arrives home, happy but penniless. Is Jack really stupid or does he have the right idea for living a happy life?

INDIA

Hodges, Margaret. *The Golden Deer*. Illustrated by Daniel San-Souci. Cambridge, Ontario: Maxwell Macmillan, 1992.

It is said that long ago Buddha came to earth many times and in many different forms. In India, he came to the city of Benares in the shape of a golden deer. This story is retold from an ancient classic, *The Jakata*. The golden deer, while protecting his herd from the hunters, brought about the freedom of all living creatures. The vibrant pictures enrich and complement the text. This book would be more suitable for seven- to eight-year-olds than for younger children. There are many stories of Buddha's visits to earth that could extend the inevitable discussions this tale will generate.

JAPAN

Compton, Patricia. *The Terrible Eek*. Illustrated by Shuta Hamanaka. New York: Simon & Schuster, 1991.

This is a Japanese folktale of misadventure retold for young children. As a young boy and his father sit huddled by their fire on a stormy night, their conversation about a terrible leak is partially overhead but distorted by the wind to "terrible eek." The chain reaction this causes throughout the forest is fast-moving and funny. The illustrations, brightly colored and whimsical, help bring the story to life.

Ishi, Momoko. Translated from Japanese by Katherine Paterson. *The Tongue-Cut Sparrow*. Illustrated by Suekichi Akaba. New York: Lodestar Books, 1987.

This well-known Japanese folktale describes what happens when greed comes between an old man and his wife. The inclusion of several onomatopoeic words in Japanese will be enjoyed by all children and will give Japanese children a chance to be knowers among their classmates.

Luenn, Nancy. *The Dragon Kite*. Illustrated by Michael Hague. New York: Harcourt Brace Jovanovich, 1982.

A crafty thief named Ishikawa learned how to construct a dragon kite so that he could steal the golden dolphin on top of the castle the Shogun built for his son. Like Robin Hood, Ishikawa steals from the rich to give to the poor. Beautifully illustrated, this delightful story also gives children some ideas about the art of making kites.

Snyder, Dianne. *The Boy of the Three Year Nap*. Illustrated by Allen Say. Boston: Houghton Mifflin, 1988.

A traditional Japanese folktale is retold by the author in simple language and a captivating style. A poor Japanese mother manages to turn the tables on her lazy son's plans for a life of ease and arrange a better life for herself. The fine lines and vivid color of the illustrations are reminiscent of Japanese painting and provide a glimpse of Japanese buildings and costumes.

Watanabe, Shigeo. *How Do I Put It On?* Illustrated by Yasuo Ohtomo. Markham, Ontario: Puffin Picture Books, 1977.

As young children laugh at Little Bear's struggles to put on his own clothes, they gain confidence in their own efforts to dress themselves.

Watkins, Yako Kawashima. *Tales from the Bamboo Grove*. Illustrated by Jean and Mou-sien Tang. New York: Bradbury Press, 1992.

This is a collection of Japanese folktales recalled from the author's childhood. Each illustration is accompanied by Japanese calligraphy for the title of each story. A wonderful collection for telling or reading and a good way to introduce children to different kinds of script.

KOREA

Harber, Frances. *The King has Donkey Ears.* Illustrated by Mary-ann Kovalski. Richmond Hill, Ontario: North Winds Press, 1986.

A fascinating story about a king who ruled in Old Korea. One morning, he awoke to find that he had grown two long don-key ears overnight. The story is reminiscent of *The Emperor's New Clothes* in Western literature. The spectacular illustrations enhance the story and present a lively glimpse of Eastern dress and artifacts.

NORTH AMERICA

Cohen, M. *Will I have a Friend?* New York: Macmillan, 1967.

On Jim's first day of school, he's worried about whether he'll find a friend. As he watches, then participates in the routines and play in the kindergarten room, he finds he can make friends and enjoy himself. A simple, effective story with mul-tiracial illustrations appropriate for children aged three to five and good for simple "show and tell" with ESL children.

Hooick-Kenyon, S. *Welcome Chao Mung.* Vancouver, British Columbia: Refugee Co-ordinating Center, 1980.

A coloring book that compares the North American and rural Vietnamese styles of living in a very simple manner. The text is written in English and in Vietnamese. Illustrations show transportation, dress, homes and shopping. Excellent for be-ginning ESL children.

Martin, Bill, Jr. *Brown Bear, Brown Bear.* Illustrated by Eric Carle.New York: Holt, Rinehart & Winston, 1970.

This delightful children's story is loaded with opportunities for practicing substitution and repetition.

McKend, H. *Moving Gives Me a Stomachache.* Windsor, Ontario: Black Moss Press, 1980.

Simple black-and-white drawings and humorous text show that moving isn't all that bad once you find something that you can call your own. Good for older preschoolers, this story helps evoke discussion of newcomers' feelings.

Relf, P. *The First Day of School*. New York: Western Publishing, 1981.

Although Elizabeth thought she was thoroughly prepared for school, she still has to adjust to new things. Suitable for all preschool ages, this book portrays a racial balance portrayed and helps ESL children review preschool routines and activities.

Toye, W. *The Loon's Necklace*. Illustrations by E. Cleaver. Oxford: Oxford University Press, 1977.

By helping an old man recover his sight, the loon receives the necklace that distinguishes it from other birds.

RUSSIA

Cech, John. *First Snow, Magic Snow*. Illustrated by Sharon McGinley-Nally. New York: Four Winds Press, 1992.

This story is based on a traditional Russian tale, *The Snow Maiden*. A lonely woodcutter molds a little girl from the first magical snow and takes her home to his wife. The child lives with them for the winter but disappears when spring comes. The heartbroken couple sets out in search of her. The colorful, whimsical illustrations have a definite flavor.

VIETNAM

Lee, Jeanne M. *Ba-Nam*. New York: Henry Holt, 1987.

Nan, a young Vietnamese girl, visits the graves of her ancestors with her family on a special day when families gather to place offerings on the graves and pray and talk together. When Nan meets Ba-Nam, the old gravekeeper, she is frightened but later, during a storm, finds that she is kind and loving.

References

LANGUAGE AND GRAMMAR

Celce-Murcia, M. & D. Larsen-Freeman. *The Grammar Book: An ESL/EFL Teacher's Course*. Rowley, Massachusetts: Newbury House, 1983.

Finegan, E. & N.Besnier. *Language: Its Structure and Use*. Toronto: Harcourt Brace Jovanovich, 1989.

Fromkin, V. & R. Rodman. *An Introduction to Language*. New York: Holt, Rinehart & Winston, 1988.

Hymes, Del. "On Communicative Competence." In *Sociolinguistics*. J. Pride & J. Holmes (Eds.) Hammondsworth, England: Penguin, 1972.

O'Grady, W. and M. Drobvolsky (Eds.). *Contemporary Linguistics Analysis: An Introduction*. Toronto, Ontario: Copp Clark Pitman, 1987.

LANGUAGE LEARNING

Bialystok, E. *Language Processing in Bilingual Children*. Cambridge: Cambridge University Press, 1991.

Chan, Itty. *Early Education in China and Its Implications in the United States*. Berkeley, California: Asian American Bilingual Center, 1977.

Cummins, J. *Bilingualism and Special Education: Issues in Assessment and Pedagogy*. Cleveland, England: Multilingual Matters, 1984.

Cummins J. "Bilingualism and the ESL Student." In *TESL Talk*. Vol. 11, no. 1 (1980).

Dale, P. *Language Development: Structure and Function*. Hinsdale, Illinois: Dryden Press, 1976.

de Villiers, P.A. & J.G. de Villiers. *Early Language*. Cambridge, Massachusetts: Harvard University Press, 1979.

Donaldson, M. *Children's Minds*. Glasgow, Scotland: William Collins, 1978.

Garvey, C. "Play with Language and Speech." In *Child Discourse*. C. Mitchell Kerner and S. Erwin-Tripp (Eds.). New York: Academic Press, 1977.

Genishi, C. & A.H. Dyson. *Language Assessment in the Early Years* . Norwood, New Jersey: Ablex Publishing, 1984.

Gleason, J.B. *The Development of Language*. 2nd Edition. Toronto: Merrill Publishing, 1989.

Klein, A. "Storybook Humour and Early Development." In *Childhood Education*. Vol. 6, no. 4 (1986).

Teale, W. & E. Sulzby (Eds.). *Emergent Literacy: Writing and Reading*. Norwood, New Jersey: Ablex Publishing, 1986.

Wells. G. *Language Development in the Pre-School Years*. Cambridge: Cambridge University Press, 1985.

Wells, G. *The Meaning-Makers: Children Learning Language and Using Language to Learn*. Portsmouth, New Hampshire: Heinemann, 1983.

Wells, G. *Learning through Interaction*. Cambridge: Cambridge University Press, 1981.

GENERAL EDUCATION

Bernstein, B. "Critique of the Concept of Compulsory Education." In *Functions of Language in the Classroom*. C.B. Cazden, D. Hymes & V.P. John (Eds.). New York: Teachers College Press, 1972.

Glenn, C.L. *Choice of Schools in Six Nations: France, Netherlands, Belgium, Britain, Canada, West Germany*. Washington, D.C.: U.S. Department of Education, Office of Educational Research and Improvement, Programs for the Improvement of Practice, 1989.

Glenn, C.L. "Putting School Choice in Place." In *Phi Delta Kappan*. Vol. 71, no. 4 (1989).

Glenn, C.L. *The Myth of the Common School*. Amherst, Massachusetts: University of Massachusetts Press, 1988.

Wittenberg, A.I. *The Prime Imperatives: Priorities in Education*. Toronto, Ontario: Clark Irwin, 1968.

Ashworth, M. *The First Step on the Longer Path: Becoming an ESL Teacher.* Markham, Ontario: Pippin Publishing, 1992.

Ashworth, M. *Beyond Methodology: Second Language Teaching and the Community.* Cambridge: Cambridge University Press, 1985.

Asselin, M., N. Pelland & J. Shapiro. *Storyworlds: Linking Minds and Imagination through Literature.* Markham, Ontario: Pippin Publishing, 1991.

Barry, M.A. & E. MacIntyre. "A Multicultural Program in a Pre-School Setting." In *Multiculturalism.* Vol. 5, no.4 (1982).

Carruthers, C. *Open the Lights.* Reading, Massachusetts: Addison-Wesley, 1982.

Chud, G. & R. Fahlman. *Early Childhood Education for a Multicultural Society.* Vancouver, British Columbia: Western Education Development Group, Faculty of Education, University of British Columbia, 1985.

Chud, G. & R. Fahlman. "Working with ESL Pre-Schoolers: Meeting the Needs of the Whole Child." In *TEAL Occasional Papers.* Vol. 7 (1983).

Cochran-Smith, M. *The Making of a Reader.* Norwood, New Jersey: Ablex Publishing, 1984.

Ellis, G. & J. Brewster. *The Storytelling Handbook for Primary Teachers.* London: Penguin, 1991.

Fahlman, R. *Multicultural Experiences for Young Children.* Reading, Massachusetts: Addison-Wesley, 1990.

Graham, C. *Jazz Chants for Children.* New York: Oxford University Press, 1979.

Gunderson, L. *ESL Literacy Instruction: A Guidebook to Theory and Practice.* Englewood Cliffs, New Jersey: Prentice Hall Regents, 1991.

Heald-Taylor, Gail. *Whole Language Strategies for ESL Students.* Toronto, Ontario: OISE Press, 1986.

Hess, N. *Headstarts: One Hundred Original Pre-Text Activities.* Harlow, England: Longman, 1991.

Mohan, B. *Language and Content*. Reading, Massachusetts: Addison-Wesley, 1986.

Rigg, P. & V.G. Allen (Eds.). *When They Don't All Speak English: Integrating the ESL Student into the Regular Classroom*. Urbana, Illinois: National Council of Teachers of English, 1989.

Scott, W.A. and L.H. Ytreberg. *Teaching English to Children*. Harlow, England: Longman, 1990.

Journals

Canadian Children: Journal of the Canadian Association for Young Children
Sue Fraser, Douglas College, P.O. Box 2503, New Westminster, B.C., Canada V3L 5B2

Canadian Journal of Research in Early Childhood Education
Ellen Jacobs, Department of Education, Concordia University, 1455 de Maisonneuve Blvd. W., Montreal, Quebec, Canada H3G 1M8

Early Childhood Research Quarterly
National Association for the Education of Young Children, 1267 Child Development & Family Studies Bldg., Purdue University, West Lafayette, Indiana, USA 47907-1267

Journal of Child Language
Cambridge University Press, London, England

Child Education
Scholastic Publications, Villiers House, Clarendon Avenue, Leamington Spa, Warwickshire, England CV32 5PR

Childhood Education
Association for Childhood Education International, 11501 Georgia Ave., Suite 315, Wheaton, Maryland, USA 20902

TESL Canada Journal
Free to members of provincial ESL associations.

TESOL Journal, TESOL Quarterly, TESOL Matters
TESOL Central Office, Suite 300, 1600 Cameron St., Alexandria, Virginia, USA 22314-2751

MORE TITLES FROM THE PIPPIN TEACHER'S LIBRARY

Helping Teachers Put Theory into Practice

STORYWORLDS: LINKING MINDS AND IMAGINATIONS
THROUGH LITERATURE
Marlene Asselin, Nadine Pelland, John Shapiro

Using literature to create rich opportunities for learning.

WHOLE LANGUAGE: PRACTICAL IDEAS
Mayling Chow, Lee Dobson, Marietta Hurst, Joy Nucich

*Down-to-earth suggestions for both shared and independent reading
and writing, with special emphasis on evaluation strategies.*

THE WHOLE LANGUAGE JOURNEY
Sara E. Lipa, Rebecca Harlin, Rosemary Lonberger

*Making the transition to a literature-based, child-centered
approach to learning.*

WRITING PORTFOLIOS:
A BRIDGE FROM TEACHING TO ASSESSMENT
Sandra Murphy, Mary Ann Smith

*How portfolios can help students become active partners
in the writing process.*

THE FIRST STEP ON THE LONGER PATH:
BECOMING AN ESL TEACHER
Mary Ashworth

*Practical ideas for helping children who are learning
English as a second language.*

SUPPORTING STRUGGLING READERS
Barbara J. Walker

*Building on struggling readers' strengths to help them broaden
their strategies for making sense of text.*

ORAL LANGUAGE FOR TODAY'S CLASSROOM
Claire Staab

*Integrating speaking and listening into the curriculum to help
children discover the power of language.*

AN EXCHANGE OF GIFTS:
A STORYTELLER'S HANDBOOK
Marion V. Ralston

Imaginative activities to enhance language programs
by promoting classroom storytelling.

THE WORD WALL: TEACHING VOCABULARY
THROUGH IMMERSION
Joseph Green

Using mural dictionaries—word lists on walls—to strengthen
children's reading, speaking and writing skills.

INFOTEXT: READING AND LEARNING
Karen M. Feathers

Classroom-tested techniques for helping students overcome
the reading problems presented by informational texts.

WRITING IN THE MIDDLE YEARS
Marion Crowhurst

Suggestions for organizing a writing workshop approach
in the classroom.

AND THEN THERE WERE TWO:
CHILDREN AND SECOND LANGUAGE LEARNING
Terry Piper

Insights into the language-learning process help
teachers understand how ESL children become bilingual.